GALÁPAGOS ISLANDS

The World's Living Laboratory

By **Karen Romano Young**

Illustrated by
Amy Grimes

What on Earth Books

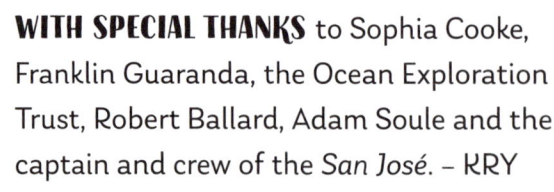

WITH SPECIAL THANKS to Sophia Cooke, Franklin Guaranda, the Ocean Exploration Trust, Robert Ballard, Adam Soule and the captain and crew of the *San José*. – KRY

What on Earth Books is an imprint of What on Earth Publishing
The Black Barn, Wickhurst Farm, Leigh, Tonbridge, Kent, TN11 8PS, United Kingdom
30 Ridge Road Unit B, Greenbelt, Maryland, 20770, United States

First published in the United Kingdom in 2024

Text copyright © 2024 Karen Romano Young
Illustrations copyright © 2024 Amy Grimes

All rights reserved. No part of this publication may be reproduced or transmitted in any form or by any means, electronic or mechanical, including photocopying, recording, or any information storage or retrieval system, without permission in writing from the publishers. Requests for permission to make copies of any part of this work should be directed to info@whatonearthbooks.com.

Written by Karen Romano Young
Illustrated by Amy Grimes

Karen Romano Young has asserted her right to be identified as author of this work and Amy Grimes has asserted her right to be identified as illustrator under the Copyright, Designs and Patents Act 1988.

Staff for this book: Nancy Feresten, Publisher; Patrick Skipworth and Laura Bullock, Editorial Directors; Andy Forshaw, Art Director; Nell Wood, Senior Designer; Rachel Lawston, Designer; Helen Peters, Indexer; Adrianne Velasco, Sophie Macintyre and Lucy Buxton, Proofreaders; Harriet Birkinshaw, Angliciser

ISBN: 9781804661147

10 9 8 7 6 5 4 3 2 1
Printed in China
DC/Foshan, China/12/2023

whatonearthbooks.com

CONTENTS

INTRODUCTION 4

Chapter One
RISING FROM THE SEABED 6

Chapter Two
ENCHANTED ISLANDS, ENCHANTED SEA 16

Chapter Three
WHEN HUMANS MADE THEIR MARK 28

Chapter Four
A TALE OF TORTOISES 40

Chapter Five
PARADISE FOR ALL 48

GLOSSARY 60

SOURCE NOTES 62

INDEX 63

INTRODUCTION

'The Galápagos is the last frontier, the best preserved place on Earth. I think every kid in the world should visit here once in their life and experience this place that is like something out of a storybook.'

Juan Pablo Muñoz-Pérez, Galápagos marine biologist, Galápagos Science Centre

Galápagos brown pelican

When I set foot on the Galápagos for the first time, I became part of a short line of people to arrive here. Short, historically, since the first humans probably arrived only 500 years ago, long after most of the rest of the world – aside from Antarctica – was full of people. Short, numerically, because not many people live here, and only a limited number are allowed to visit.

The Galápagos National Park covers the entire group of 21 islands and lots of little islets. (That sounds big, but all of the land together is only as big as the island of Puerto Rico in the Caribbean Sea.) Just five of the islands have people living on them (Isabela, Santa Cruz, Floreana, San Cristóbal and Baltra), and the total population of 30,000 would fill only a third of a big football stadium. People live on only three per cent of the land. The other 97 per cent – and the ocean surrounding it – has been set aside for special protection by the entire world.

Why? These islands are the setting for a natural experiment that has taught us how life starts, shifts shape and restarts, and the setting for a new experiment that might light the way forwards for the rest of the world.

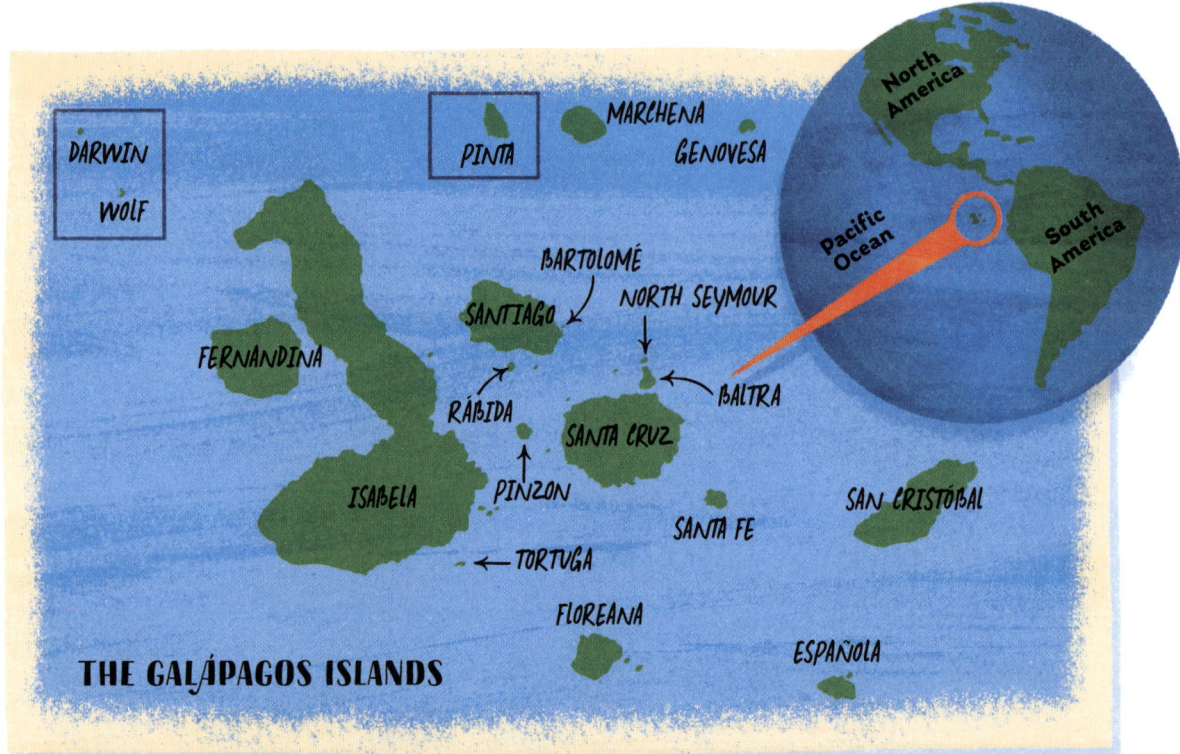

THE GALÁPAGOS ISLANDS

Galápagos Ecological Airport, on Baltra Island, is the world's first 'green' airport, powered entirely by sun and wind. Shutters open and close to keep the temperature comfortable, and the water is supplied by the island's desalination plant (which takes the salt out of seawater to make freshwater).

Chapter One
RISING FROM THE SEABED

'Let's talk about the union that humans and animals can have, how they can protect each other and help each other, and how they need each other.'

Sophia Cooke, conservationist, Galápagos Conservation Trust

After my plane landed on Baltra Island, I climbed aboard a medium-sized tour boat called the *San José* and met 13 other tourists from around the world, half a dozen Ecuadorian crew and tour guide Franklin Guaranda, who grew up here. There are no bridges among the Galápagos Islands. And even on a single island, volcanoes and rough terrain keep people from moving around. Any visit here involves boats – from tiny inflatable Zodiacs to big research ships. The *San José* has room for eating, sleeping, small meetings and relaxing, without the laboratories of research vessels or the hot tubs that cruise ships have.

The *San José*

Each day on the *San José*, Franklin asked our group to do challenging things – and we always said yes. That's how we found ourselves climbing one ancient volcano and descending inside another; swimming with penguins, iguanas and sharks; boating in caves of birds and bats; looking at skeletons in lava holes; visiting baby tortoises; hiking in pirate territory; and so much more. Suntanned and sleepy by the time we climbed into bed, we snoozed with our doors open to the bright rays of the moon and the lullaby of the sea.

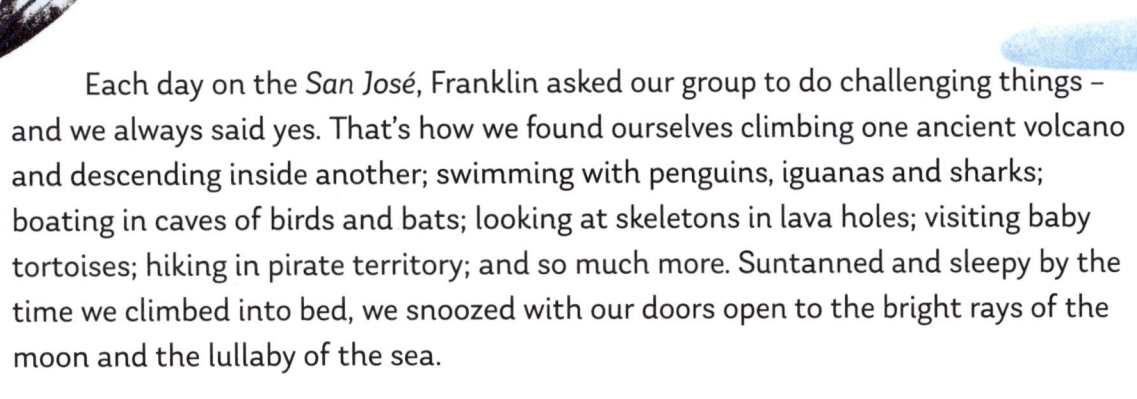

A Zodiac

One morning found my new friends and me creeping down a slimy stone staircase and trekking through Cueva del Cascajo. This cavelike lava tube was forged by a channel of molten lava that cooled into hard rock from the outside in. As the lava drained out, it left a nearly three-kilometre tunnel behind – slippery, dank, dripping, dotted with puddles and just high and wide enough for adventurers to walk, stoop or squeeze through.

Franklin told our group stories of other lava tubes – some as wide as ten metres, some full of seawater and inhabited by whitetip reef sharks. The sharky tubes could only be explored by a combination of rock climbing, caving and snorkelling (they weren't on our itinerary, so I felt safe saying I'd like to visit!). Not far away, we stood on the edge of Los Gemelos (The Twins), massive pit craters that formed when lava flowed out of underground pockets and the ground above them collapsed into two enormous sinkholes. At more than 700 metres deep, either one could fit the world's second-tallest building, the 128-storey Shanghai Tower, with more than 60 metres to spare.

Welcome to Santa Cruz island, which rises abruptly from seacoast to mountain, with a basement full of old lava tubes, forests shaped by lava cells that have burst like bubbles and an attic of misty highlands. Situated roughly in the centre of the archipelago (island group), it's middle-aged compared to the older islands to the east and the newer ones to the west. It's also home to a town of 18,000 people and the headquarters of the Galápagos National Park Service.

FRANKLIN GUARANDA AND A TROOP OF TOURISTS (INCLUDING VISITING BIRDS)

Franklin is a naturalist and a National Park Ranger. Only Galapagueños – people born here or married to someone who was – can hold this job. Besides guiding tours and keeping people safe, Franklin monitors the health of the places he visits and the wildlife there. He's so expert that he can tell when something doesn't belong. He was the first person ever to sight a dolphin gull in the Galápagos – a bird usually found off the coast of southern Argentina and Chile 5,000 km away.

Dolphin gull

The Galápagos archipelago is a work in progress. Earth's oceans and continents all ride atop massive pieces of crust called tectonic plates, greased from underneath by a layer of melted rock called magma. Hot spots occur where deep wells of magma push up, punching through the crust to form undersea volcanoes. Over millions of years, the magma (called lava when it reaches the Earth's surface) flows out of these volcanoes and builds up into seamounts, undersea mountains that eventually nose up out of the sea as islands. That's what happened, and is still happening, here.

The Galápagos hot spot* formed around 23 million years ago where a plume of heat from beneath the seabed pressed the Earth's crust up, forming a volcano. About 1,600 kilometres from the hot spot, two side-by-side plates – the Cocos and Nazca Plates – continually split apart, opening a seam in the ocean floor called the Galápagos Rift. As magma oozes up to fill the seam, it solidifies into rock, forming new ocean floor – and pushing the Nazca plate slowly east-southeast towards Ecuador at a rate of four centimetres a year.

The hot spot doesn't move – the land moves over it. As the plates of the Earth's crust are carried away from the hot spot, old islands crumble into the sea to the east and new ones emerge over the hot spot to the west. Española, the southeasternmost island, is among the oldest at three to four million years old – but only among the islands with their tops to the sky. East of Española lies the Carnegie Ridge, a chain of ancient islands sunk in the sea. Fernandina, to the west, is the youngest island, just 700,000 years old. And that's where we were headed next.

* It's called a hot 'spot' but is actually 150 kilometres wide.

LIVING ON LAVA

When I wrote this book, La Cumbre (The Top), the active volcano on the island of Fernandina, had last blown its top on the 12th of January 2020, erupting for nine hours. Glowing veins of lava poured down its slopes from a crack 1,300–1,400 metres high – the third eruption in three years. How often does it erupt on average? Before the set of three in 2017, 2018 and 2020, it last blew in 2009. We know about those four eruptions from satellite images, but it is harder to pin down how often La Cumbre blew before we could observe the Earth from space. Nobody lives near enough to see it happen.

Fernandina's caldera, a bowl six kilometres wide and 850 metres deep*, changes shape and depth as lava floods into and flows out of the volcano. Between eruptions, shrubs and cacti grow and bloom, and lakes form in the craters. At least once, in 1968, an eruption dropped the caldera about 300 metres, sucking down the lake. Its ducks went with it.

* As wide as 550 telegraph poles laid end to end and deep enough to stand two Shards on top of one another inside with lots of room to spare.

Some 90 per cent of the world's volcanic activity happens where tectonic plates meet, either pulling apart or sliding on top of one another. The edge of the Pacific Ocean has so much tectonic activity and so many volcanoes that it is known as the Ring of Fire (though it's more of an upside-down U than an O). But hot spot islands such as the Galápagos and the Hawaiian Islands aren't part of that ring because hot spots are under the plates and push volcanoes through them.

From the Fernandina shore, our tour group progressed across snaky ropes of pahoehoe lava (fun to walk on, like balancing on a network of twisting kerbstones), careful to avoid the marine iguanas that we sometimes wished were a little more afraid of us. As we hiked on, the lava changed to collapses, chopped up chunks, and boulders – 'A'ā lava. (It's said people walking on it say, 'agh! agh!' because of the difficulty.) The park service lays out paths across the lava, revising them regularly to reroute hikers around danger zones, with a stop sign at the point where continuing would lead you too close to the volcano, with its caldera and crevices. The skeletons of those that fell in (iguanas, sea lions) leer up like neon warnings.

The ring of fire (shaded in orange) is an area of volcanic activity up to about about 500 kilometres wide, running for 40,000 kilometres along the edges of the Pacific Ocean. The dots on this map represent areas of volcanic activity.

IN THE DEEPEST PART OF THE SEA

Picking my way across fields of lava, I couldn't help wondering what the ship E/V *Nautilus*, scientist Bob Ballard and the ROV *Hercules* were seeing at the exact same moment deep in the Pacific Ocean that surrounds the islands.*

Right here in 1977, on an expedition Ballard helped lead, people riding in the human-operated vehicle *Alvin* had discovered a part of the natural world nobody knew existed: a hydrothermal** vent later named Rose Garden because it was so full of life.

Their discovery changed the scientific story of life on Earth. Before scientists riding in *Alvin* found the Rose Garden, every food chain on the planet seemed to rely on a plant or plankton that processed sunlight into food through photosynthesis. This was the way life worked, or so we thought. Since the seafloor was too deep for the sun to reach, scientists assumed it must be a desert devoid of life: without food, you couldn't have a food chain, right?

* E/V stands for 'exploration vehicle', a kind of ship. ROV stands for 'remotely operated vehicle', a small remote-controlled submarine.
** Hydrothermal means having to do with warm or hot water.

THE CORPS OF EXPLORATION MEETS THE WORLD

The Ocean Exploration Trust's Corps of Exploration – made up of people from 18 to 80 – includes scientists, ROV pilots, navigators, camera and video operators, communicators and students. Their job is to be the eyes and ears of people ashore while they work aboard E/V *Nautilus* to visit and map sites on the seafloor. Through telepresence – audio, video and live interactions – they share their experience with people in offices, labs, schools and homes worldwide. In turn, folks ashore share their knowledge and questions to contribute to the discoveries from afar.

Then scientists traced a strange warm wisp of ocean water back to its source in the seabed, and they discovered something truly incredible. The crack in the seafloor – the first hydrothermal vent discovered – spewed heat and chemical food to support a strange group of alien creatures. Ballard and the other scientists examined long tubeworms with skins like spaghetti and tips like lips, anchored to rock. With them lived blind crabs, giant clams and mussels, floating colonies of creatures like dandelion blossoms and more. Nobody had ever seen these creatures before. How could they exist here? What were they living on? Why didn't the deep sea chemicals poison them?

Back then, nearly 20 years before texts and emails, people on shore had to wait for reporters to get the news over radio from the ship before they could hear about the life-changing discovery of the Rose Garden. By the time I was visiting the Galápagos, vents had been discovered all over the sea. Camera images travelled from sub to ship via fibre-optic cables, and satellites beamed them – and the exclamations of excited scientists – back to shore.

ROV *Hercules*

A vent chimney builds up quickly as hot liquid minerals cool and solidify.

Giant tube worms

Vent crabs can't see well.

Giant mussels

Now Ballard and a new crew were back in the Galápagos to map the Rose Garden with *Nautilus'* extra-detailed multibeam sonar. With all the new technology, folks all over the world could look over the shoulders of people aboard the ship as they monitored the ROV *Hercules* on the ocean floor. The other *San José* passengers and I watched too, recently back aboard after a morning of following marine iguanas. I was seeing the action on my computer screen just as I might have from home, but it was exciting to know that *Hercules* was not far from where I sat in the lounge of the *San José*, just a lot deeper in the sea.

When *Hercules* reached the location of the Rose Garden, the high-definition camera revealed nothing but old, dead shells and lifeless basalt (lava that solidifies as it cools). That busy and beautiful otherworldly place was long gone.

Giant tube worms, like many vent animals, harbor bacteria that turn vent chemicals to nutrients.

Dandelion siphonopheres may look like flowers, but they are really colonies of tiny creatures, like a hive of bees or a coral reef.

Pompeii worms are named after the Italian city ruined by lava from the volcano Vesuvius; they tolerate the very hot water coming out of the vent.

Vampyroteuthis infernalis, the Latin name of the **vampire squid**, means 'vampire squid from hell', thanks to its reddish colour and its home in the abyss.

The ROV pilot steered the sub onwards, her hand on the joystick, waiting for a glimmer of hope. Gloomily, the scientists peered at the camera screens. Then Ballard, along with the others, began to shout. 'There! That way! Tube worms! Vent crabs! Giant mussels!' The Rose Garden had lost its bloom and died out, but now a tiny new vent that researchers had named Rosebud back in 2002 had blossomed into a new garden. It was just one of the things that made the ocean around the Galápagos seem as enchanted (and as fragile) as the islands themselves.

The things that look like elephant ears on a *Cirrothauma murrayi* **octopus** are actually fins.

Like many creatures that live in the dark layers of the sea, **comb jellies** produce light, possibly as a form of defence, to lure prey or to communicate.

Alvinocarid shrimp are named after the submersible *Alvin*, which carried the explorers who located the Rose Garden.

An **eelpout** looks like an eel but isn't one. It's a long thin fish with no scales.

Chapter Two
ENCHANTED ISLANDS, ENCHANTED SEA

'The chief sound of life here is a hiss.'

Herman Melville, *The Encantadas, or Enchanted Isles*

Once it had begun to emerge – molten, magnificent – from a sea that teemed with life, this chain of islands got seeded, and forests and meadows grew. Somehow, even though the Galápagos were a very long flight or swim from any shore, mothers, fathers, eggs, spores and babies showed up and populated the slopes of the volcanoes.

Once, these arrivals were lonely pioneers; now the islands are home to multitudes. And new life forms, some found nowhere else on Earth, developed from the ones that arrived here from far away. This is a hot spot for biodiversity, with an exceptional variety of species found on the islands themselves and in the water around them.

Biodiversity is higher on the Galápagos than in many other places because there are so many different habitats, places where life can thrive on particular foods, water sources and places to sleep and mate. Endemic species – those found

only in the Galápagos — make up most of the indigenous* land birds, mammals and reptiles — and around a third of the indigenous land plants. And that's a uniquely big deal to scientists working to understand how life, well, lives.

SOME KNOWN INDIGENOUS SPECIES OF THE GALÁPAGOS	Indigenous species	Endemic species	More info
All plants and animals	about 5,000	about 1,900	61 species are critically endangered.
Plants	more than 600	more than 200	There are also more than 800 species of plants that humans have introduced to the islands.
Fish	more than 530	79	30 species of shark, including the whale shark, prowl the waters of the Galápagos.
Land birds	39	27	The endemic species include 17 species of Darwin's finch and 4 mockingbird species.
Reptiles	39	35	The endemic species include 12 species of Galápagos giant tortoise, the Galápagos marine iguana, 3 species of land iguana, 9 species of lava lizard, 4 land snake species and 6 gecko species.
Mammals	8	7	The endemic species include 1 seal species, 1 sea lion species, 4 species of rice rat and 1 bat species. Some 1 to 2 dozen whale and dolphin species can also be found here.
Sea birds	more than 20	7	The endemic species are the Galápagos penguin, the flightless cormorant, the waved albatross, the lava gull, the swallow-tailed gull, the Galápagos petrel and the Galápagos shearwater.

* *Indigenous species were here when humans arrived. Endemic species were here when humans arrived, plus don't live anywhere else in the world. So all endemic species are indigenous but not all indigenous species are endemic.*

The **Bryde's whale** doesn't raise its flukes (tail) when it dives.

The largest **manta rays** have a wingspan of more than six metres and can weigh more than 2,700 kilograms, more than a hippopotamus.

Snorkelling off the shores of Fernandina, Franklin showed us whitetip reef sharks hanging out at the bottom of a lagoon ... then seahorses ... and a red-lipped batfish, which was like something out of an animated cartoon. Galápagos penguins and sea lions kept darting past, paying no attention to us human swimmers. Incredible! When a marine iguana swam by, its tail lashing, its limbs hanging loose, I sputtered with laughter and swallowed a salty mouthful. I bobbed to the surface, pushed back my snorkel mask and took a deep breath. The glory of this place overwhelmed me.

In the little inflatable boats called Zodiacs we floated in coves lined with caves, cliffs streaked with old lava tubes, outcroppings where blue-footed boobies nested and boulders dotted with dark, diving birds with strange, useless wings.

Ages ago, flightless cormorants settled here. Now they are found only on western Isabela and Fernandina, making them one of the rarest birds in the world. With no land predators and with plenty of fish to catch in the water, the birds didn't need to fly. Over many years, the cormorants that used their wings less became more streamlined, able to dart through the water in pursuit of prey. So they did better in the competition to mate and have young. Generation upon generation, the wings shrank, all the better to fish.

We travelled west aboard the *San José*. After an hour, we spotted a school of hundreds of young hammerhead sharks, a Bryde's whale – an unusual sighting! – and to me the most unforgettable thing of all: a pod of manta rays, swimming past whip-fast and leaping high out of the ocean. They spun as they leaped, somersaulting by the hundreds to flash a white belly and black back. When they fell, they belly-flopped and back-slapped down as if they were in a contest to see who could make the biggest noise and the hairiest splash. (The behaviour may actually be a mating call.) Why was everything here so exceptional?

Marine iguanas don't have gills, but they can hold their breath for half an hour, possibly more.

The Galápagos sea lion may also be seen sleeping on park benches and promenades, challenging humans for space.

THERE MUST BE SOMETHING IN THE WATER

Why are Fernandina Island's western waters so full of life? Currents from every direction meet here. A current is like a motorway of water in the sea. The South Equatorial Current arrives from South America. The Humboldt Current flows in from the south; the Panama Current comes in from the tropical north; and the Cromwell Current arrives from the west.

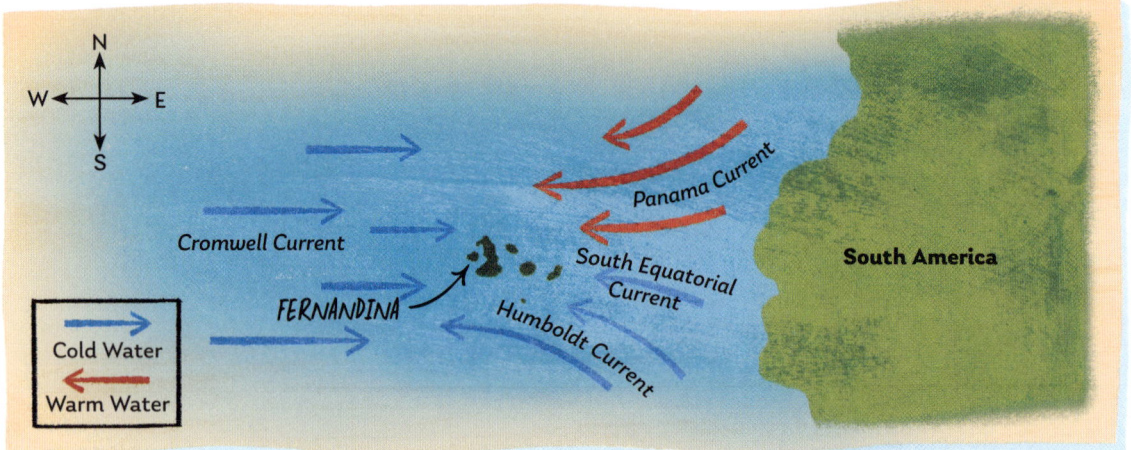

What's more, the Cromwell and Humboldt Currents both flow hard against the edge of the Galápagos submarine platform, a thickening of the Earth's crust on which the islands sit. As they hit that edge, they force up cold water full of nutrition* from the deep sea. This process is called upwelling, and it feeds the bottom of the food chain that supports the multitudes of eaters that thrive here.

But there's something else hidden beneath the sea that contributes to Galápagos life – undersea volcanoes. New volcanoes on their way to the surface and old ones – former islands – are hidden below the water. These seamounts are yet another Galápagos environment incredibly rich in life. 'We'd go along the sandy, muddy seabed and see a fish here or there,' scientist Adam Soule says. 'Then we'd get onto the seamounts and they were just covered with life – corals, fish, anemones, sea stars.' Seamounts are the underlying reason for some long-established fishing holes, so they're crucial to the life of the islands.

Mapping them is key to preserving this life; knowing exactly where the seamounts lie will allow Galapagueños to ensure the source of so much life will be carefully managed so it won't be destroyed.

*Upwelling nutrition is mostly minerals and organic matter (animal poop or the remains of dead organisms). It feeds the surface phytoplankton on which the whole food chain relies.

King angelfish

ADAM SOULE, PELAYO SALINAS DE LEÓN AND A DEEP-DIVING BUBBLE

In 2015, Adam Soule, a submarine volcanologist from Woods Hole Oceanographic Institution (USA) led an international team, including Pelayo Salinas de León of the Charles Darwin Foundation, to become the first to map the seamounts of the Galápagos Platform, the thick slab of the Earth's crust on which the archipelago sits. Their ship, M/V Alucia, carried two submersibles and used multibeam sonar (sound signals that bounce off undersea surfaces to create depth data) to create maps of the seafloor more detailed than had ever been made before. Adam Soule was one of the researchers who dived in the submersible Deep Rover 2. He says, 'We recognised that we were seeing stepping stones that used to be between the islands, seamounts that were above sea level in the past, with tops cobbled with stones like the island beaches have now. And we've only mapped about five per cent of what's under the sea.'

The *Deep Rover 2*'s spherical viewing space allows its two pilots to see almost all the way around them.

Yellowtail surgeonfish

Kelp

21

THE WORLD OCEAN – FOR SHARKS, FISH AND THE REST OF US

Travellers in the past told tales of sailing the seven seas, but now we recognise that there is only one world ocean. Atlantic, Pacific, Arctic and Indian Oceans share the same water, which circulates through them on a worldwide 'conveyor belt' powered by the rise and fall of layers of warm and cold water. Yes, the Galápagos waters are protected, but currents from elsewhere flow in - carrying warming, more acidic, waters and rubbish, and admitting fishing fleets from around the world.

Warm water to the north washes over coral reefs said to be several thousand years old. Coral reefs produce 25 per cent of the world's marine species, maybe more. So keeping the coral reefs healthy is crucial to the health of the Galápagos fishery.

Fishing is big business, and fishing fleets from around the world know that if they wait just outside the Galápagos Marine Reserve, the fish will come to them.

JORGE RAMIREZ-GONZÁLEZ AND THE FISH MARKET

Jorge Ramirez-González is a Mexican-born marine biologist and senior fisheries scientist with the Charles Darwin Foundation. His lifelong study of fisheries helps him understand — and plan for the future of — the Galápagos fishery.

His work involves not only biology and ecology, but also studies of people — how fishing is done here, how rules about it are set and how to balance people's needs with those of fish, from sea cucumbers to sharks.

Fishing is an important lifeline for people in the Galápagos. The fishery here employs 500 fishers and provides food for the island's residents and many visitors. What do people fish for here? Around 50 species, including lobster, squid, sea cucumbers, fin fishes, sharks and rays.

The local fishers are not alone here. Outsiders aren't allowed to fish in the Galápagos Marine Reserve, but the big schools above the seamounts lure fishing boats from as far away as China. These ships sit outside the border of the reserve and wait for fish to cross the line. They're killing more fish here than can be replaced to feed people on the other side of the ocean.

Managing the Galápagos fishery is a challenge because it's not an all-or-nothing activity. The goal is to allow fishing now but also to make sure there are plenty of fish around for the fishers of tomorrow. Step one in maintaining the fishery is to make sure every creature on the food chain has a healthy population and a safe environment. Step two is using fishing technology that lets fish thrive, while letting fishers thrive at the same time. Among the experiments are fish aggregating devices (FADs). These buoys attract tuna, swordfish and other food fish away from their breeding grounds. The buoys send fish numbers via satellite to local fishers, so they can catch fish without disturbing their babies. The hope is that this will help sustain the population of fish for the long term.

The Galápagos are a haven for sharks. In recent years, worldwide shark populations have dropped more than 90 per cent. Much of this drop has been caused by humans who kill the sharks for their fins*, and by fishers who accidentally

* Soup made from shark fins is a delicacy in many places in Asia.

DIANA ALEXANDRA PAZMIÑO JARAMILLO AND ILLEGALLY-CAUGHT SHARKS

Diana Alexandra Pazmiño Jaramillo, a shark scientist from the University of San Francisco de Quito, Ecuador, focuses on shark forensics – detective work on the bodies of sharks taken from foreign fishing boats that shows whether they were caught legally or not. Her clue-checking process involves DNA and can be used to enforce shark fishing rules in other parts of the world, protecting endangered sharks.

Hammerhead sharks visit the coral to get personal clean-up services from the reef fish that pick parasites off them.

catch sharks when seeking other fish. The Galápagos Islands are one of the few sites in the world where shark populations are healthy. Pelayo Salinas de León, a marine ecologist at the Charles Darwin Foundation, found that the islands Darwin and Wolf are home to the world's largest biomass of sharks, which means the most sharks in an area its size anywhere in the world. So, shark scientists working here have a unique study opportunity.

There are so many sharks partly because the reserve protects them, but also partly because tourists come here to dive with sharks, making them more valuable alive than dead. Each live shark is worth £300,000 a year to the local economy, according to Pelayo, so no local tries to kill them.

In May 2020, the organisation Mission Blue announced a new Hope Spot – an underwater animal highway called the Cocos-Galápagos Swimway. They hoped it would become an international marine reserve linking the Galápagos with the coast of Costa Rica. A year later, the MigraMar expedition, a group of scientists from six countries, followed the 2,930-kilometre migratory path themselves. They observed whales, sharks, sea turtles and other migrators. What for? To help increase understanding of the importance of this part of the ocean – and to provide information to leaders with the power to protect the East Pacific.

Potholes at the edge of the sea are often edged by dainty, brightly coloured crabs on tiptoe. Their reflections are mirrored in the water: red legs, orange-gold-rose backs, with dashes of bright blue. These are **Sally Lightfoot crabs**, so called because they can scoot across the surface of the water without sinking. Like most animals on these islands, they aren't scared of people unless they think you're about to step on them.

PELAYO SALINAS DE LEÓN TRACKS SHARKS FROM SPACE

Charles Darwin Foundation lead shark and fisheries scientist Pelayo Salinas de León tags pregnant hammerhead sharks with satellite tags in order to track their migrations.

Among his other projects, he identified a new species of cat shark during the 2015 _Alucia_ expedition. (You can read about other scientists on that journey on pages 20–21.)

MARINE IGUANAS: OLDER THAN THE HILLS

Hiking shoes are required here: the island of Fernandina is home to the Galápagos' largest marine iguana colony, and if the natives had been feeling active, we might have got our feet tangled with their claws. But the iguanas were sunning themselves as usual, leaving space for hikers. So we trekked along the black lava, passing the huge white bones of a whale beached long ago. Suddenly everything went into motion as a big shadow winged its way over us. A Galápagos hawk swooped, low and curious. Horrified, we ducked, then whirled to watch it snatch and carry off a big lump of coal with legs – an unlucky marine iguana. Then we noticed an iguana skeleton that had been picked clean.

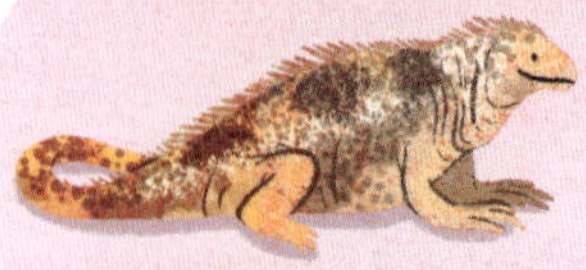

Santa Fe land iguana
found only on Santa Fe Island

Marine iguanas are sun worshippers. Each dawn, sleepy and chilled, they turn their sides towards the rising sun, the better to maximise solar heat and energy. As they warm, they turn again, pointing their snouts towards the sun to control their inner thermostats. When they're fully baked, their stomachs call time, and they slide into the sea in search of seaweed to eat.

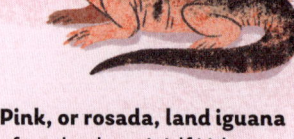

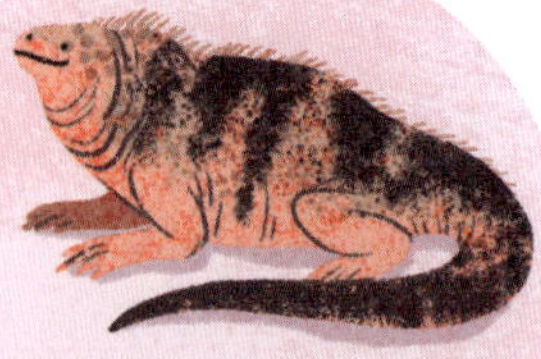

Pink, or rosada, land iguana
found only on Wolf Volcano on Isabela Island

These grey-black iguanas have family nearby: land iguanas in yellow, orange and pink. Uncannily like the dragons of legend, they lay their eggs at the edge of volcanic craters.

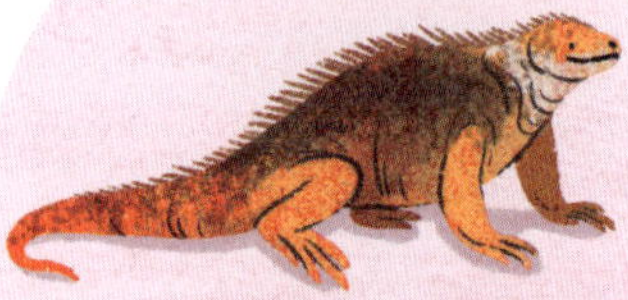

Galápagos land iguana

How did all these sturdy lizards reach such remote islands in the first place? There are no eyewitnesses, but scientists have patched together a story that tells how the first reptiles got to the Galápagos Islands. Over time, a few tortoises, iguanas, lizards and snakes must have got stranded in a snarl of leaves and sticks on the mainland, then swept along down a river to the sea, and gradually carried here on a current.

Generation after generation, the iguanas branched off from the original settlers, divided between land and sea. What's more, they did so before the islands arose in their present form. The marine iguanas must have used their newfound swimming ability to colonise newly surfaced islands while the old ones sank behind them. They're literally older than the hills.

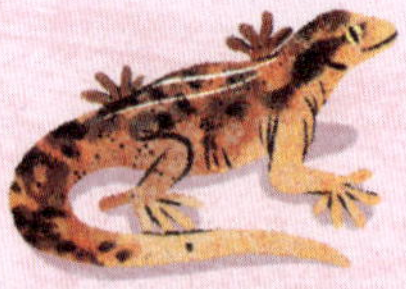

Galápagos leaf-toed gecko

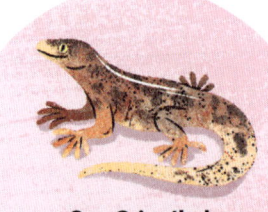

San Cristóbal leaf-toed gecko
found only on San Cristóbal Island

JUAN PABLO MUÑOZ-PÉREZ AND THE MARINE IGUANA

Juan Pablo Muñoz-Pérez, called JP, is an Ecuadorian scientist who makes the islands his home – and his laboratory. He wants to know what the marine iguana gave up to gain its seawater wizardry. After all, the marine iguana's body and the way it moves aren't that different from its closest mainland relatives, the black spiny-tailed iguana and the green iguana found in Ecuador. What's missing is speed. Marine iguanas may glide and dart through the water, but on land they're slow. JP thinks this may reveal why mainland iguanas and lizards haven't made a similar transition to the sea: in environments with predators, this lack of speed would work against them.

Salt glands in extended nostrils remove sea salt from its bloodstream; it sneezes and snorts to expel the salt. White glop all over its head is the sea salt snot that didn't spray far enough away.

Lava lizards are often found sitting on top of something or someone, such as a marine iguana; they change colour when threatened.

MARINE IGUANA
The only lizard in the world that makes its living in the sea. Some are more than 1.2 metres long.

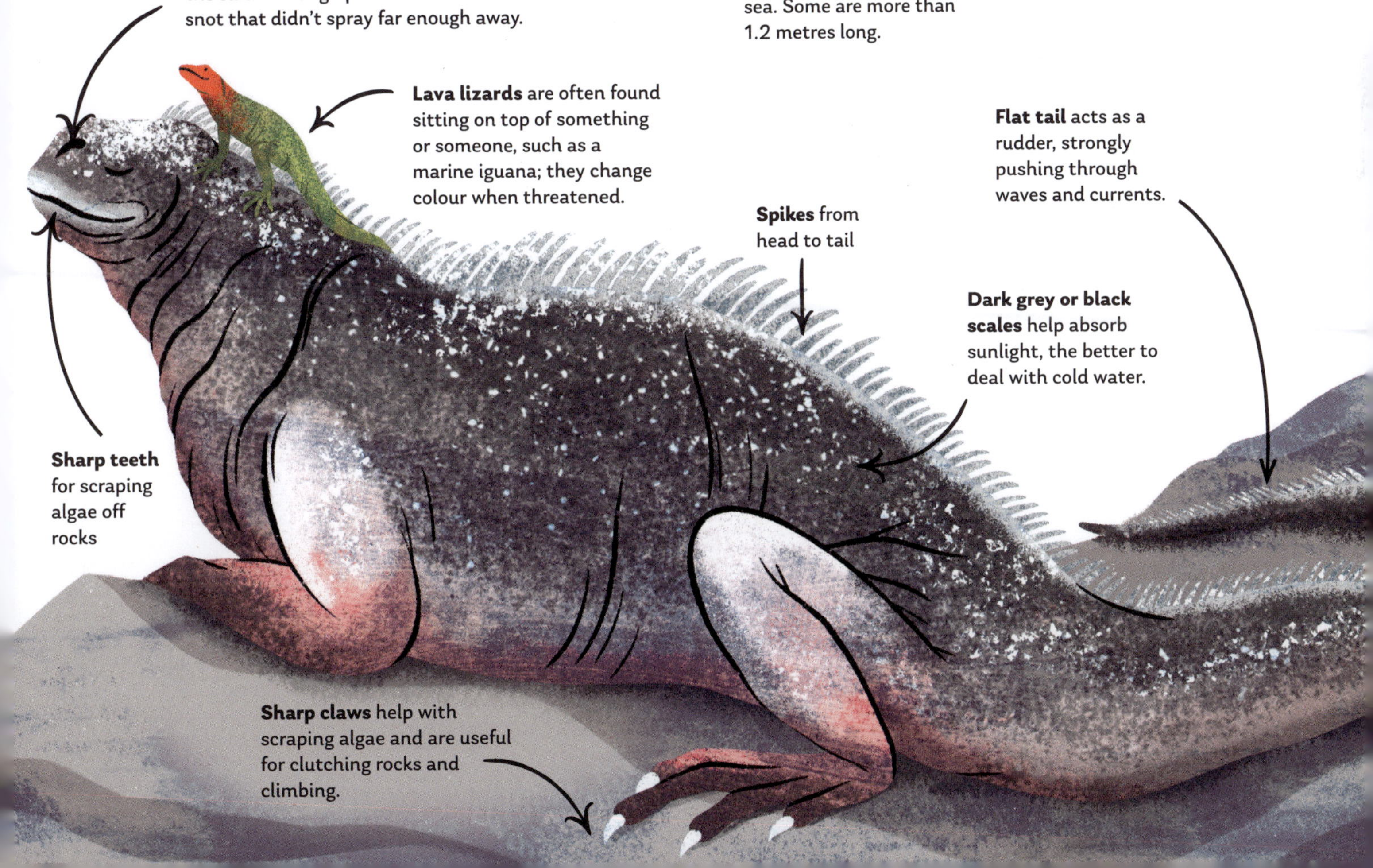

Spikes from head to tail

Flat tail acts as a rudder, strongly pushing through waves and currents.

Dark grey or black scales help absorb sunlight, the better to deal with cold water.

Sharp teeth for scraping algae off rocks

Sharp claws help with scraping algae and are useful for clutching rocks and climbing.

Chapter Three
WHEN HUMANS MADE THEIR MARK

'By far the most remarkable feature ... [is] that the different islands ... are inhabited by a different set of beings.'

Charles Darwin, *The Voyage of the Beagle*, September, 1835

The captain steered the *San José* into Tagus Cove, Isabela Island. If the high cliffs surrounding the cove could talk, they would shout the names of the human visitors scrawled on their rocks. Pirates, whalers and navy sailors even carved and painted their ships' names.

You can't visit the Galápagos Islands without seeing signs of their most famous visitor. No, the rocks above Tagus Cove do not say CHARLES DARWIN WAS HERE. But the lake we climbed past was named for the British naturalist. And in Puerto Ayora, the main town of Santa Cruz island, his face was on T-shirts, his name was on signs, and the research centre named after him contributes new understandings of nature to the world – just as he did in his time.

Today was the day for the tour group to climb Isabela's volcanoes and pass Lake Darwin. The path wove among incense-scented palo santo (holy stick) trees, through dry brush and cacti, into a tangle of shrubs where closely-woven nests were practically camouflaged – though Franklin skilfully pointed them out.

The birders among us went crazy: the hill was alive with the sound of finches, individuals representing some of the 17 or so species found only here (the exact number is a matter of debate)*. Unafraid of us, a finch perched closer than I'd ever seen a bird, and every one of us snapped its picture.

These 'Darwin's finches' didn't just branch off from their ancestor long ago but continue to change to meet the conditions of their niches. They're doing it right now, as I'm writing this. Maybe the conditions have produced seeds with thick, hard shells. The finches that will do best are those with beaks that can handle those seeds. By the time you're reading this, in the future, tiny seeds might have become abundant, and finches with thin beaks – best for picking seeds out of cracks and crevices – will eat better. And those who eat better will be more successful at mating, lay more eggs, and hatch more chicks – chicks with tough or tiny beaks, depending on their parents.

As the *San José* group climbed Darwin Volcano, you might say that Darwinian data was all around us. Here on Isabela every volcano once had its own giant tortoise species, separated by the lava flows. The volcano stopped them just as it now stopped us hiking up the trail. Looking over Darwin Volcano, we could see Wolf beyond, with its streamer of smoke and steam. It was still cooling from its eruption just a few weeks before our trip. We turned back towards the sea.

* Different scientists recognise different species of finch. The Charles Darwin Foundation lists 17: small ground finch, medium ground finch, large ground finch, sharp-beaked ground finch, Genovesa ground finch, vampire finch, common catus finch, Española cactus finch, Genovesa cactus finch, small tree finch, medium tree finch, large tree finch, woodpecker finch, mangrove finch, vegetarian finch, green warbler finch and grey warbler finch. You can see some of them on the next page.

Lake Darwin, a saltwater lagoon, formed inside a tuff cone, a chimney off Darwin Volcano.

Vampire finch

Small tree finch

Medium ground finch

Large tree finch

CHARLES DARWIN AND A FASCINATION WITH FINCHES

Charles Darwin sailed into San Cristóbal aboard HMS Beagle on the 17th of September 1835. Settlers from Ecuador had arrived in the islands only a few years earlier. (They officially became part of Ecuador in 1832.)

Darwin recognised the extraordinary weirdness of Galápagos animals and plants. He tried to imagine their origins, along with analysing what made them similar to – but oddly different from – plants and animals with which he was familiar. The wildlife seemed to have somehow changed from those familiar forms, as though their design was tweaked to improve the way they fit into the local food chain and environment. Yes, there were tortoises elsewhere in the world, but these were different. And, the settlers told him, the tortoises from one island were different to those from another. It was Darwin who, intrigued and observant, zoomed in on differences in one animal – a finch – from one island to the next.

But Darwin almost missed the point. As he gathered specimens of finches to take home for study, he neglected to note which island they came from. Only later, using finches others had brought home, did he piece the story together. The more Darwin studied, the more he understood: finch beaks altered not just island to island, but mountain to shore; not just according to location, but according to available food; not just to available food but to conditions of heat and moisture that led to food availability.

As Darwin zeroed in on what caused finches to change, the Galápagos Islands became the laboratory for his theory about how all life everywhere adjusted and tweaked in order to improve its chances of surviving and thriving. The individuals with the best characteristics for finding whatever food was available lived healthier lives and reproduced, while weaker individuals with the wrong tools were weeded out by nature. So, nature selected the ones

Medium tree finch

Woodpecker finch

Common cactus finch

Grey warbler finch

Small ground finch

that would win – and, on the flip side, eliminated the losers, sometimes even leading to the extinction of species.

Darwin's theory was published in 1859 as the book <u>On the Origin of Species by Means of Natural Selection</u>. It had taken him decades after his 1835 visit to sort out what he was seeing in his five weeks' worth of notes, sketches and samples. His observations were evidence of a huge natural experiment. It seemed as if a giant scientist had popped islands down in the middle of the ocean to see what would happen – what life forms would show up, and how they would evolve, changing in response to new conditions.

What's more, it had taken time for Darwin to accept what he was seeing and understanding – that nature selected the living things with the best characteristics for their niches, which led to species changes. In other words, evolution. In the 19th century, the stories that scientists began telling – based on their concrete observations in the field – bumped hard up against the Bible's creation stories. The ideas that the Earth had existed for longer than a few thousand years, and that animals had changed over time were impossible for many people to accept.

In describing this theory of evolution based on natural selection, Darwin knew that he wasn't just reporting on a scientific discovery; he was breaking with tradition – and, some would say, with God.

Many people still wrestle with the idea that science reports on the world, even if that report doesn't match up with their religion's creation story, timeline or version of how things happened. Others say that whatever story science tells is a story of God's creation. Then there is the idea that the world works according to natural laws ... or are 'natural laws' just another way of saying God? Darwin didn't have the answer to this, but he shaped his story to his facts, the data about the animals and plants that he watched, examined and spent the rest of his life working to understand.

Green warbler finch

Large cactus finch

Large ground finch

Mangrove finch

THE ORIGIN OF SPECIES

A century and a half after Darwin published his famous theory, British scientists Peter and Rosemary Grant and their colleagues figured out that Darwin's finches descended from one ancestor that had arrived in the islands within the last two million years. Responding to the conditions in the niches they spread to, the birds radiated – branched off – showing different characteristics and behaviours. This adaptive radiation happens most often when animals find new niches that don't have predators. Different finches adapted to feed on cactus flowers, seeds of various sizes and even the blood of other birds – and iguanas.

Yes, Darwin saw the beak adaptations, but he didn't recognise the extent of radiation – how many new species it led to. More evidence came in 2015, when the Grants analysed bird DNA – the genetic material that passes the 'plan' for beaks and other characteristics from parent to chick.*

* DNA contains the recipe for building and operating a living thing and is carried in the cells of all organisms on Earth. The ALX1 gene the Grants analysed also relates to face and skull characteristics in humans – and may have something to do with the differences in our looks.

PETER AND ROSEMARY GRANT AND A NICHE PLACE TO VISIT

Beginning in 1973 and continuing for the next 40 years, scientists Peter and Rosemary Grant lived on the little island Daphne Major, camping in caves and tents and catching, measuring and describing finches. The released finches went back to their regular lives of eating everything they could get their beaks around – a diet that differed depending on available food and on the characteristics of their beaks – and the Grants added that information to a database. Over time, they watched evolution by natural selection happen in real time. The Grants were able to link big-beak seasons (such as 1977) to drought, and soft-seed seasons to wetter events created by the likes of the 1982–1983 El Niño, a warm-water trend in the Pacific. Their answer to the question of what they know that Darwin didn't? 'Genetics!' That's the science of heredity – what gets passed down to offspring, and the changes in DNA (mutations) that allow evolution to happen.

HUMANS MOVE IN

There's a feeling among the experts that the Galápagos would have been a far different place if it were nearer the South American coast – and within easier reach of human hunters and settlers. Its isolation is a main reason that the islands are the way they are: not overly developed, a living laboratory where the impact of the environment on its species can be observed as it happens.

The first human known to have made it to the Galápagos Islands was the Bishop of Panama, Tomás de Berlanga, who arrived in 1535. The Spanish word galápago means tortoise or land turtle, and it also means 'saddle' – a reference to the shape of the animals' carapace (shell), which is what gives some people the idea of riding them. What's so important about these tortoises that a whole island chain is named for them? And what about the marine iguanas, Galápagos penguins, flightless cormorants, candelabra cactus, 'sunflower' trees – don't they count for anything?

These other endemic animals and plants may be astonishing, but they weren't reason enough to sail your ship all the way here, at least 1,000 kilometres from anywhere. But giant tortoises were. Intrigued by the name, ships' captains sailing through the South Pacific made 'the Tortoise Islands' an important stop-off point.

Voyagers pulled up to the islands, refreshed their water and stocked up on handy, though heavy, portable food: giant tortoises.

Those drawn here by the promise of food (and good hiding places) included 17th-century pirates. They mapped the islands in detail and catalogued some of the animals (especially the useful or edible ones). Still today, 'pieces of eight' – Spanish coins that pirates often stole from the ships they captured – are sometimes found on Galápagos beaches.

By the time Darwin visited, Ecuadorians had established a settlement on the island of Floreana. It wasn't easy to make a living here. (It still isn't.) For one thing, there is very little fresh water. Desalination operations (which take the salt out of seawater), farms, dyeing businesses and fisheries were among the first businesses to try to put down roots here. Whaling – a massive industry in Darwin's time – thrived off the coast, where the cold, chock-full-of-food waters put the islands on the migration map for many whale species. But the first whaling station here was a flop. How settlers struggled on these dry, salty islands!

Pirates made their livings by stealing cargo from other ships – and needed to make island stops as much as their targets did.

From the 1830s to the 1950s, the Galápagos' population included exiles: prisoners banished here. It was common practice during those decades for convicts to be forced to do labour, sometimes on farms such as sugar plantations that couldn't be sustained if they actually paid the workers, and sometimes to waste time doing projects like the 'Wall of Tears,' constructed of lava rocks that served little purpose other than punishment. It wouldn't be until 1959 that the penal colonies – work camps for criminals from mainland Ecuador – were shut down at last. It was the same year that the islands were set aside as a national park.

The Panama Canal opened in 1914, creating a passage between the Atlantic and Pacific Oceans. This made it easier to travel to the Galápagos from Europe. Several countries grew interested in establishing military footholds here. Around this time, small groups of Norwegian and German settlers arrived to develop fishing and build a cannery for processing fish for export.

And then there was science. Darwin inspired a new generation of scientists who wanted to get to the heart of the evolution story. The California Academy of Sciences sponsored many early expeditions. The scientists who took part in the first of these, led by Rollo Beck in 1905, thought that the Galápagos species were on the way to becoming extinct. They took home 70,000 specimens of plants and animals so they would not be forgotten! It was a time when natural historians set the goal of collecting for their museums; Beck was known for his speed at stuffing a bird to preserve it for display. Though scientific methods have changed since, the Academy still houses the world's largest collection of Galápagos samples, including preserved finches, which provide important information to researchers to this day.

The year 1925 saw the arrival of divers from the New York Zoological Society, who returned with samples of deep sea fish, plankton and hundreds of photographs documenting the discovery of new species. In 1932, Templeton Crocker led the second Academy expedition as part of a worldwide cruise in his sailboat, *Zaca*. In the 1960s, the Galápagos International Scientific Project started the Charles Darwin Research Station on Academy Bay on Santa Cruz Island and established the Galápagos as a living museum – and laboratory. Discoveries made by scientists at these research institutions and others have changed our understanding of the whole world and its history.

Did anyone visit the Galápagos before the 1500s? Archaeologists have investigated the possibility. The Inca civilization of South America was the closest ancient empire to the Galápagos, but it seems unlikely they ever made it there; the Inca weren't known for being sailors. But Thor Heyerdahl, who visited in 1952-53, believed he had found clues that people from South America who came before the ancient Inca may have visited here. Archaeologists with his expedition found 130 pieces of pots and other ceramics. Heyerdahl and his crew had sailed from Peru to

In the late 1800s and early 1900s, Floreana Island was home to the Hacienda el Progreso, a sugar plantation. Many of the workers there were unhoused people from big cities in Ecuador or had been arrested for crimes there. The government forced them to move (usually with their families) to this remote island and to be entirely controlled by the plantation owner, as if they were enslaved.

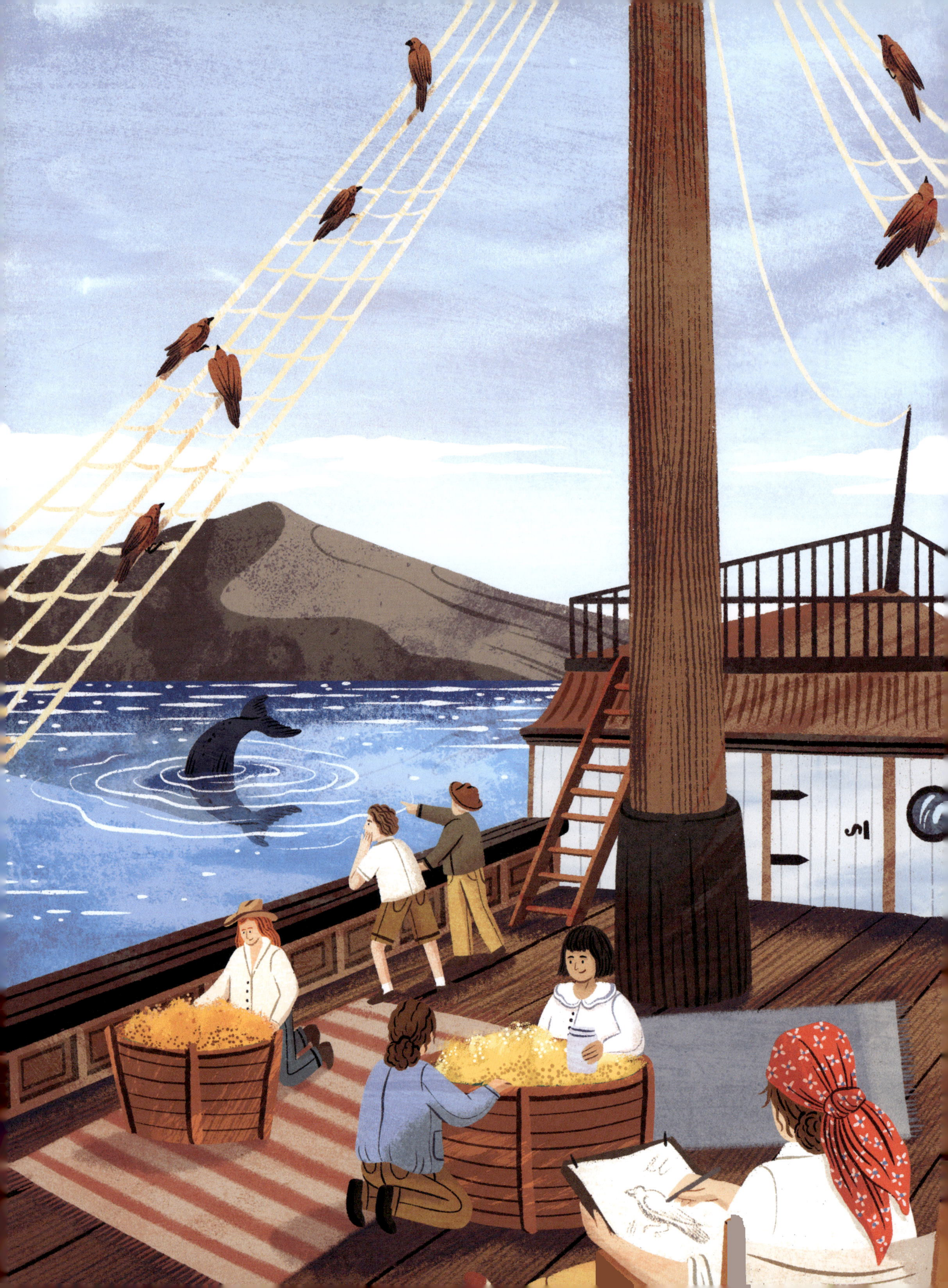

Polynesia five years before in a boat made the way some indigenous South Americans made theirs, demonstrating that these ancient people had the technology to make the trip.*

Today, humans living in the Galápagos Islands represent a variety of heritages. Some are descendants of frontier settlers from Ecuador. Some are – or followed in the footsteps of – researchers investigating the living lab. There are as many reasons to live in the Galápagos as there are people. Because it's home. Because of science. Because of tourism. Or all three. Most of the 30,000 people who make their homes here are involved in science, tourism or service industries: they fish, farm, teach, lead tours, run restaurants or shops, service boats and provide other crucial services.

The diverse people of the Galápagos have one thing in common, though. They know that the future of these islands depends on them and their visitors and how they use this amazing environment – or lose it. Although the islands are remote and isolated, the challenges all Earthlings face have arrived on these shores. And, because the Galápagos are small, they make a perfect place to test Earth-saving methods. The archipelago stands for the rest of the world: could what works here work elsewhere?

* Some archaeologists disagree with Heyerdahl that ancient South Americans visited the Galápagos. The Australian researcher Simon Haberle examined the collection Heyerdahl found and wasn't convinced. The collection is housed at the Charles Darwin Research Station on Santa Cruz Island.

FRANCESCA CUNNINGHAME AND BIRGIT FESSL AND THE LAST 100 MANGROVE FINCHES

These Charles Darwin Foundation researchers tell the story of mangrove finches, the rarest birds in the Galápagos. The finches live on Isabela Island in a small patch of mangrove forest. The birds' nests are threatened by black rats, as well as vampire flies. Both predators were 'introduced,' meaning they are not native to Isabela. At times the researchers give the baby birds a head start by gathering eggs and chicks, raising them in captivity until they can (hopefully) fend for themselves, then releasing them into the wild.

Chapter Four
A TALE OF TORTOISES

'Amigos de las Tortugas: este club ecológica la formamos algunos niños de la isla Isabela ... Trabajamos para ayudarlas.'

('Friends of the Tortoises: this ecology club was created by children of Isabela Island ... We work to help them.')

Message at Centro de Crianza, Isabela's giant tortoise breeding centre

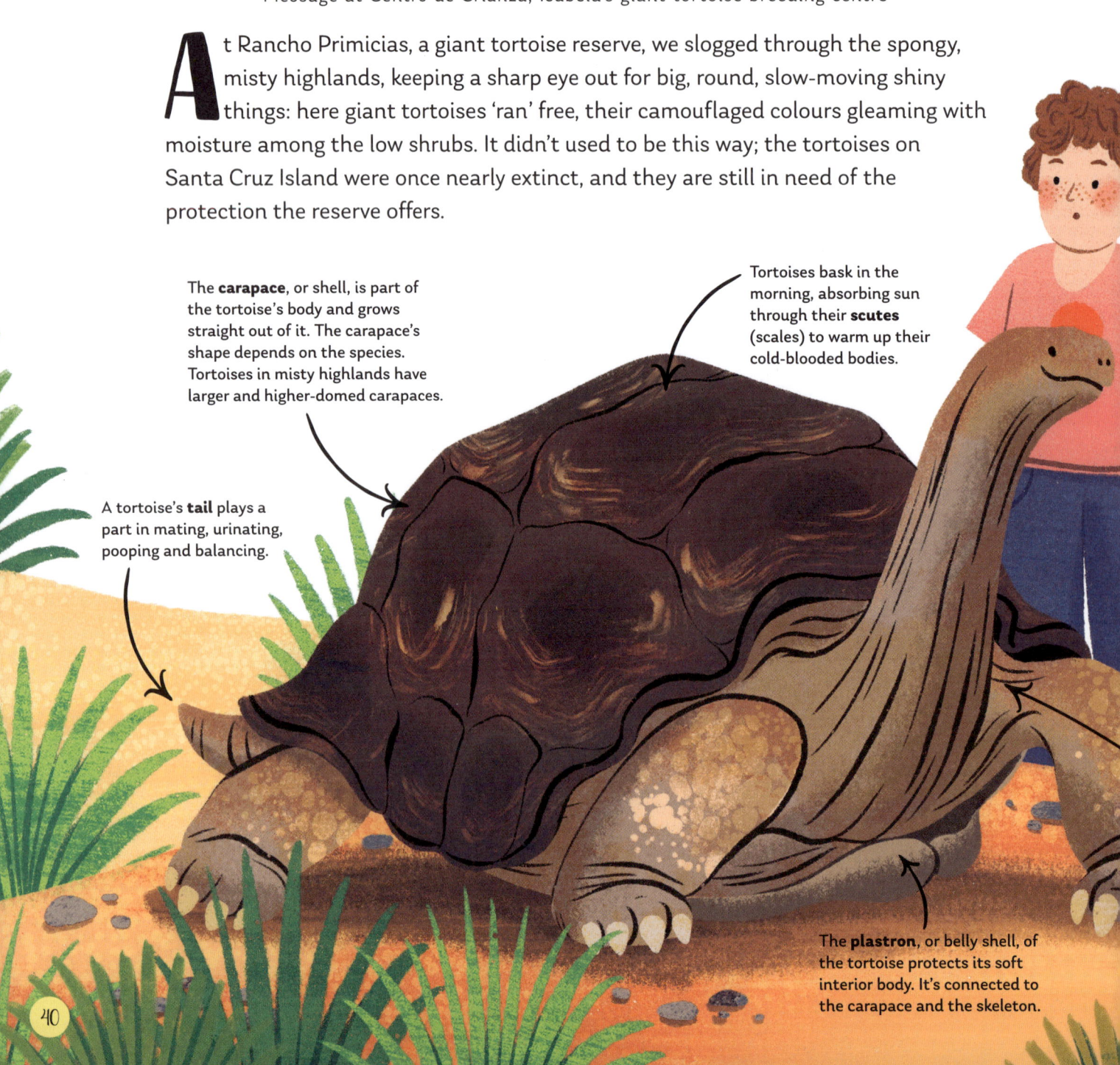

At Rancho Primicias, a giant tortoise reserve, we slogged through the spongy, misty highlands, keeping a sharp eye out for big, round, slow-moving shiny things: here giant tortoises 'ran' free, their camouflaged colours gleaming with moisture among the low shrubs. It didn't used to be this way; the tortoises on Santa Cruz Island were once nearly extinct, and they are still in need of the protection the reserve offers.

The **carapace**, or shell, is part of the tortoise's body and grows straight out of it. The carapace's shape depends on the species. Tortoises in misty highlands have larger and higher-domed carapaces.

Tortoises bask in the morning, absorbing sun through their **scutes** (scales) to warm up their cold-blooded bodies.

A tortoise's **tail** plays a part in mating, urinating, pooping and balancing.

The **plastron**, or belly shell, of the tortoise protects its soft interior body. It's connected to the carapace and the skeleton.

The Galápagos giant tortoises are remarkable. They can live to be well over 100 years old, much older than all but the longest-lived humans. The oldest one we know of lived to be over 170. The largest Galápagos tortoises (which are usually males) can reach 1.8 metres long and weight more than 250 kilograms.

These tortoises are a big success story, with 20,000 to 25,000 giant tortoises in the wild. This is a lot fewer than the 250,000 of the 1500s, but much more than the dangerously low population of the 1970s, when they looked in danger of vanishing altogether. Even with this sucess, three giant tortoise species may be extinct, including *Chelonoidis abingdonii*, the Pinta Island tortoise, of which Lonesome George, who died in 2012, was the last. The other two died out from Floreana and Santa Fe islands.

Fernando Franco of Centro de Crianza

Tortoises living in the highlands have shorter **necks**, and those in the lowlands have longer ones. There's a gap between their shell and neck, which suggests they had no predators while they were evolving.

Tortoises in dry lowlands have smaller, **saddle-shaped carapaces.** This form allows the tortoise's neck to be longer, helping it to reach up to find lowland food such as prickly pear cacti.

Like other reptiles, giant tortoises arrived in the Galápagos Islands by sea. They found an ecosystem with plenty of food and not a single animal to prey on them. Over time, tortoises on different islands – and even different areas on the same island – began to change to suit their niches. While giant tortoises died out on the mainland of South America, preyed on by humans and other animals alike, Galápagos tortoises thrived.

Take Isabela, for example: the big island's 100-kilometre backbone is a fusion of six volcanoes. The five active ones – Wolf, the tallest at 1,707 metres, Darwin, Alcedo, Sierra Negra and Cerro Azul – surround themselves with fields of lava every few years, decades or centuries. The eruptions are usually rare enough to give soil time to accumulate and plants time to establish themselves – but not rare enough for these areas to combine and form a shared environment. The result: boundaries between volcanoes that tortoises can't cross. So, Isabela didn't just develop its own species of tortoise, it developed five.

Since the arrival of the very first humans, it's been challenging to be a giant tortoise. Humans took one look and saw food – lots of it and easy to catch. The tortoises were hunted down by the hundreds, loaded alive into ships and taken away. Since they could live a long time without food and water, they could be stored and eaten when the sailors were ready.*

GOATS VS TORTOISES

Alcedo Volcano's shrubbed slope was long home to its own particular giant tortoises – but more recently it hosted a hundred thousand goats. As people arrived, they brought new species with them on purpose (goats, blackberry plants) or by accident (rats and insects stowed away on ships). These, like the species that drifted or blew here, took advantage of niches – even if that meant taking over from the endemic animals.

It was the US Navy ship *Essex* that brought the first goats to the Galápagos Islands in 1813. The crew released the goats to graze overnight and had trouble getting them back aboard the next day. That was bad news for the giant tortoises – also grazers. Over the years, the goat family expanded. Running wild, they ate the food giant tortoises relied on and trampled the lands where the leaves and fronds grew. Tortoise populations fell and kept falling.

---

* Tortoises have slow metabolisms, meaning they use water, food energy and warmth slowly. This allows them to go up to a year without eating or drinking.

Chelonoidis becki

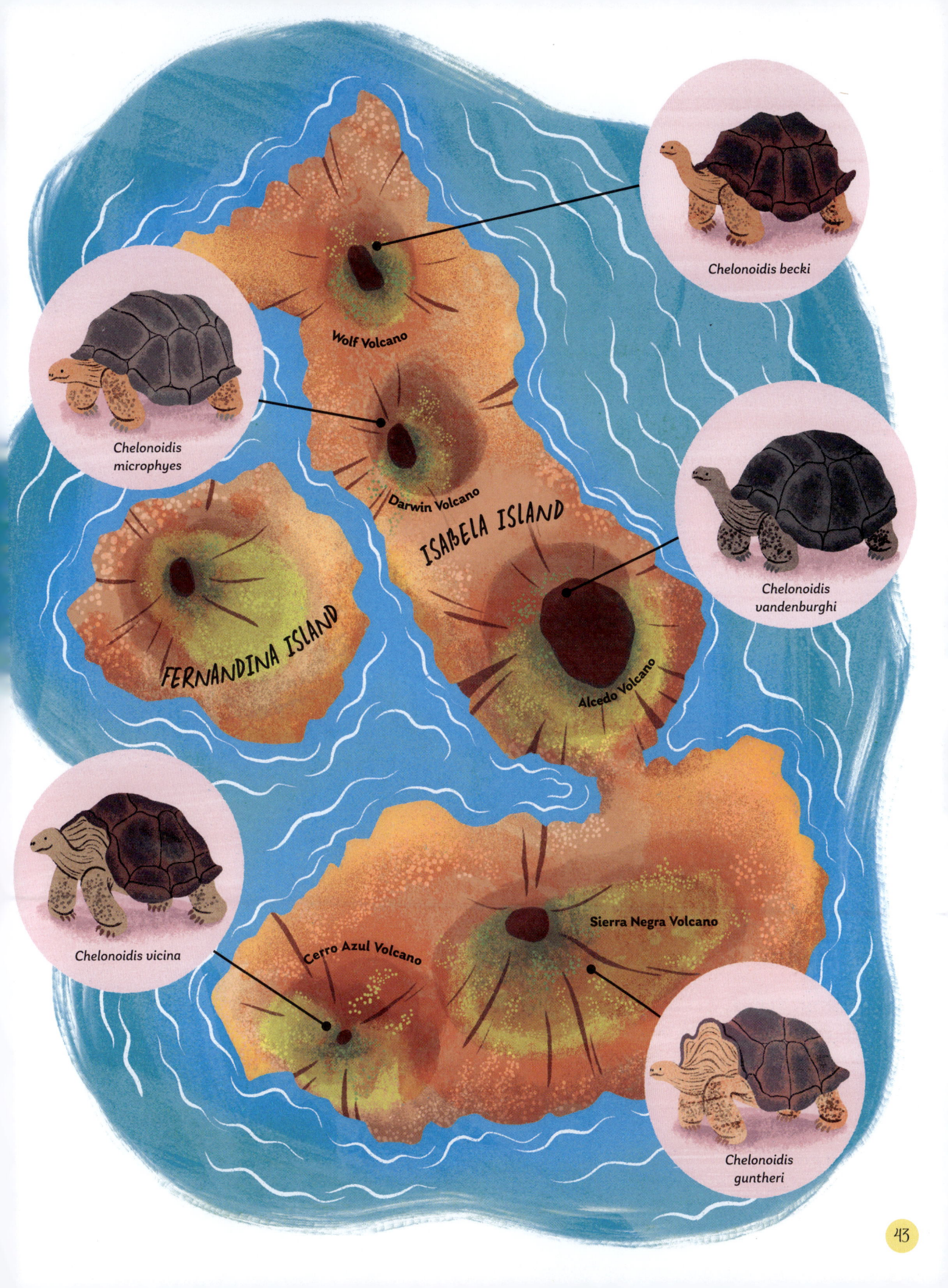

Chelonoidis microphyes

Wolf Volcano

Darwin Volcano

ISABELA ISLAND

Chelonoidis vandenburghi

FERNANDINA ISLAND

Alcedo Volcano

Chelonoidis vicina

Cerro Azul Volcano

Sierra Negra Volcano

Chelonoidis guntheri

43

In 1997, officials targeted the goats and other domesticated animals gone wild. They hired hunters to shoot them from helicopters. Some 80,000 goats were killed on Santiago Island and 60,000 on Isabela Island – as well as thousands of pigs. By 2021, Wacho Tapia, director of the Giant Tortoise Restoration Initiative, reported that the Alcedo tortoises numbered 15,000 – up from 6,000 during the reign of the goats.

Now that introduced livestock are under control, breeding programmes are releasing young tortoises into the wild by the hundreds. At Centro de Crianza Tortugas Gigantes Arnaldo Tupiza Chamaidan, Isabela's tortoise breeding centre, Fernando Franco introduced us to tortoises from tiny to titanic: incubators of eggs give way to hatchlings, then progressively older and larger tortoises. Last were enclosures for adult tortoises the breeders hoped would mate. Some tortoises were already making the effort, one big boulder-shaped body perching atop another.

Other recent projects have been designed to help tortoises' relationships with people – and their cats, their dogs, their cars, their roads. The tortoise experiments in the Galápagos have yielded a recipe for success (and examples of failure) for conservationists elsewhere in the world who are working to save and restore endemic species. Rhinoceros, pandas and tigers are just a few of the animals whose loss would be an unspeakable shame for the world – and whose conservationists look to the Galápagos for inspiration.

Part of the success has come from people changing their behaviour towards animals. Instead of eating tortoises – or relying on imported animals that eat tortoise habitat – people here began making money from tourists, who are more likely to visit because there are amazing animals to see.

Having so many conservationists in the community has helped the tortoises and all the other plants and animals, too. It allows residents and visitors to come together to understand the Galápagos environment and to develop practices that could benefit more world ecosystems and their animal and human inhabitants. That's a big improvement from the attitudes of the first people who came to the islands ready to take and use whatever they found, even if they used it up.

LINDA CAYOT AND A HELICOPTER-LOAD OF TORTOISES

Scientist Linda Cayot (who died in 2022, a few years after I spoke with her) helped design the Isabela tortoise breeding centre in the late 1980s. She remembered being there in 1994, when a helicopter arrived. Its precious cargo: tortoises from Cerro Paloma, the western shoulder of the Sierra Negra Volcano. This population was close to disappearing, down to just a few adults, some of which were flown here. 'It was the biggest success story, at least for me,' Linda said. Just ten adult tortoises formed the Cerro Paloma breeding group. 'Today the centre abounds with hundreds of their offspring,' Linda told me, 'I couldn't stop smiling as I walked around the enclosures, remembering when there were only a few left.' When tortoises are old enough to survive in the wild, they are released.

GEORGE AND FERNANDA

Giant tortoises were extinct on Pinta Island – or so everybody thought. But then in 1971 a scientist came upon Lonesome George, a Pinta tortoise and the last of his species. A reward of 10,000 US dollars was offered to anyone who could find George a mate, searching not only Pinta Island, but everywhere else, including zoos around the world. No such luck. Zoologists encouraged George to mate with females from other species, hoping to get a hybrid (half-Pinta, half something else) and keep the line going, but no luck with this either. After George died in 2012, scientists studying tortoises at Wolf Volcano, on Isabela, realised that some of them were actually half-Pinta hybrids. How could this have happened? One theory is that long ago whalers set loose Pinta tortoises, throwing them overboard – and they drifted to Isabela. So now zoologists want those tortoises to mate to bring back the Pinta species. So far? No luck with this plan either.

In May 2021, a blood test confirmed that a giant female tortoise found on Fernandina Island was *Chelonoidis phantasticus*, the Fernandina Giant Tortoise. Only one had ever been found before – a male found 112 years earlier. At that time, experts figured he was the last of his kind, his species made extinct by volcanic eruptions. And yet … here's Fernanda! The Galápagos National Park Directorate and

Lonesome George

Fernanda

the Galápagos Conservancy made an expedition to Fernandina in March 2022 to begin the hunt for a mate for Fernanda – whom they hoped wouldn't meet the fate of Lonesome George. The tortoise hunters had seen tracks and scat (tortoise poo) that gave them hope they'd find one or two.

Eighteen people combed Fernandina for Mr Right, covering 65 square kilometres of territory ridged with hard, sharp lava flows, scanning every leaf for telltale bites. They found nothing. They held onto hope that a new search – from a helicopter – might still find a mate for Fernanda. It didn't. But scientists point out that Fernanda herself doubled the all-time count of Fernandina tortoises (from one to two) – a hopeful sign in itself.

AINOA NIETO AND TORTOISES TRACKED FROM SPACE

Ainoa Nieto, a wildlife veterinarian at the Charles Darwin Foundation, hovers over newly hatched tortoises to attach satellite tracking devices to their shells – then uses the signals the devices send to map where the babies go, identifying the pathways they take from the nest to the niche where they'll find food, shelter and mates. The goal of the project is to learn tortoise migration patterns and paths on Española, Isabela and Santa Cruz Islands – and to use the information to help make decisions about what people can and cannot put within those paths, including farms, roads and other barriers.

Chapter Five
PARADISE FOR ALL

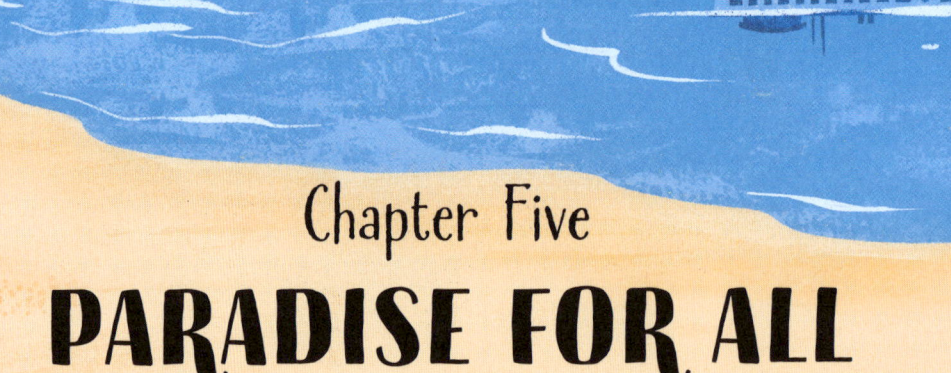

'There's a lot of people trying to make a better world for the kids, but I would say it could be also good to make better kids for our world. Education is a big key to making people change.'

Toto Idrovo, surfer and volunteer with Juan
Pablo Muñoz-Pérez's plastics research programme

Many people say the Galápagos Islands are on the 'bucket list' of places they dream of travelling to in their lifetimes. By 2019, an average 250,000 visitors were coming each year – more than eight times the number of residents. The *San José* was one of a fleet of 74 tour boats. The nearly 300 hotels were stuffed full. Too many people? Not, some say, if the tourists bring in money that can be spent to protect and care for the islands. The Charles Darwin Foundation reported that 43 per cent of the Galápagos economy came from tourism.

We tourists were learning about the islands, taking away any rubbish we produced and trying to tread lightly, not straying off the hiking trails. How could we be a problem? For one thing, we all needed food, water and electricity – stressing systems that were already strained serving the people who live here. Besides, consider some scary scenarios: lights from a tour boat like the *San José* could attract insects from one island, and the boat could transport them to another – where they could act as an invasive species. And what if a tour boat – or a container ship bringing supplies – were to have an oil spill?

PRECIOUS GEM

In the early 1930s, Ecuador enacted the first laws to protect wildlife in the Galápagos. Soon after, World War II got underway, bringing more people here. Before World War II, the only way to get to the Galápagos was by sea. During the war, an air force base was built on Baltra Island – and when the war ended, the airport remained. This was before many tourists came to the island to explore and have fun. Now it's the way most people arrive – tourists, scientists and other guests.

Most of the islands' visitors have an interest in seeing and experiencing this exotic place, whether they're adventurers, divers or birders and animal lovers (like my tour group). Scientists from away come, like the ones on E/V *Nautilus* at the Galápagos Rift. They may arrive for temporary stays while they do research, or may live here for good and work on projects for the Galápagos Conservancy, the Charles Darwin Foundation or another research institution.

In 1959 – a century after the publication of *On the Origin of Species by Means of Natural Selection* – the entire archipelago was designated a national park. This was when 97 per cent of the land was set aside for conservation. The boom in boat tours began ten years later. Air travel had made the world a smaller place, easier to get around. Thus, the Galápagos Islands were no longer something as vague as a sea monster on a map. In 1973, the archipelago became a province of Ecuador. The world had begun to pay attention to the Galápagos gem.

In 1978, the islands became a United Nations Educational, Scientific and Cultural Organisation (UNESCO) World Heritage Site, and was later joined by other treasured sites, including India's Taj Mahal, Chile's Rapa Nui National Park (Easter Island) and the USA's Statue of Liberty. In 1984, the archipelago was added to UNESCO's Man and the Biosphere programme, establishing it as a 'learning base' – a miniature model of the world ecosystem where practices could be developed that might be helpful elsewhere. The idea is that people's lives can be improved in a sustainable way – in other words, while taking care of the environment at the same time.

MARÍA JOSÉ REICHENBACH GETTING KIDS INTO NATURE

María José Reichenbach (Majo for short) leads El Mangle (The Mangrove), an agile learning community – one of just two across Ecuador – that supports play and project-based learning (learning through experiences) for children and teens from 4 to 18 years old. Majo helped create the Galápagos' new teaching plan that fosters local understanding, pride, ability and responsibility in the kids who will run things here in the future. She says the programme has helped teachers get a clearer idea of what sustainability is, and how it can happen here.

Of course, the Galápagos environment includes the surrounding ocean. In 1986, the Galápagos Marine Resources Reserve was established to protect the seas, and in 2001, the marine reserve was added to the World Heritage Site. The Reserve covers 138,000 square kilometres of sea. In 1990, it became a sanctuary for whales.

In 2010, new goals were set to get the islands off the list of endangered ecosystems. Instead of just trying to preserve what they had, islanders made specific plans for a sustainable future. But the future of the Galápagos is often at odds with the present. Sometimes it seems as if what is good for the environment is bad for the people and the other way around.

For the environment: Limit the number of people who can visit and immigrate.
For people: Tourism brings money into the local economy, and people are needed to work in the tourism industry.
For the environment: Set limits on fishing.
For people: Many citizens make a living from fishing.
For the environment: Plan for energy production and use, improve water quality and farm food locally to decrease the need to import food.
For people: Many citizens find working in tourism easier than farming. And it's hard to make long-term plans because leaders – and what they'll pay for – change often.
For the environment: Respond to changes caused by global warming and pollution.
For people: Making these changes costs a lot of money.

So, the islands need tourism money, but tourists add to the pressures on the environment, and fixing the environment costs money … and around it goes.

Then, during the 2019–2022 Covid-19 pandemic, tourism ground to a halt, putting the islands in dire financial straits. Yet people looked around at the way things were without the tourists and began thinking about how to restructure their system to make things better when the tourists came back.

As the islanders struggled to survive the steep drop in income, conservationists helped find money to start programmes designed to improve the natural environment and also the local living conditions. These programmes ranged from cleaning up lingering effects of a 2019 oil spill at San Cristóbal Island, to building local athletic facilities, to starting new farm co-ops so more people could eat locally grown food. All those programmes employ Galapagueños, many of whom had lost their tourism jobs.

At the same time, the community changed what kids in the Galápagos learn at school and elsewhere. In past years, students followed the Ecuadorian curriculum, with little in it about their home. The new curriculum includes the history of the Galápagos and its special place in science. New programmes take kids to the remote exciting sites that typically only tourists can afford to reach, building ability, understanding and pride.

Extracurriculars matter, too. Noemi d'Ozouville piloted Galápagos Infinito to take Year 7 students to the ocean and teach them to swim. Diana Alexandra Pazmiño Jaramillo of the Galápagos Science Centre and other women scientists created the Gills Club for local girls. They take the girls to observe manta rays and their nursery areas (which need protecting) and teach them to use microscopes to assess samples.

Manta rays

COMING CLIMATE CHANGES

People in the Galápagos care as much about climate change as people anywhere else, maybe more, because this small region, so dependent on the sea, can experience a big impact. In addition, across conservation, education and government, Galapagueños and visitors are working to come up with small-scale solutions that may work as models for larger communities elsewhere.

Fossil fuels such as gas and oil are the major cause of global warming and climate change. The islands aim to bring fossil fuel use to zero. In 2007, the first wind turbines were installed on San Cristóbal. Some generators were switched to run on oil from the physic nut, grown in Ecuador, rather than fossil fuels. Among other plans for decreasing fossil fuel use is increasing solar power.

Here in the Galápagos, as elsewhere, sea levels will rise. So will sea temperatures. The sea will become more acidic as it is forced to absorb more carbon dioxide, the waste product of fossil fuels. This weakens the shells of animals, including corals. Coral shells make up coral reefs – on which many of the world's fish species depend.

Galápagos mangrove forests store carbon dioxide, too. If they drown because of sea level rise, that function will be lost, tipping the balance to even more extra CO_2. This imbalance and the changes in sea temperatures will result in stronger weather trends. Big storms will grow bigger, more violent, more destructive and more frequent.

El Niño* events, which create warm trends every few years, could show up more and more often, with a bad effect on sea lions, penguins and other seabirds. El Niño years – like oceanic heat waves – starve Galápagos penguins because they disrupt the cold water that brings them food. During the 1997–1998 El Niño,

---

* El Niño is part of a climate pattern known as ENSO, or the El Niño Southern Oscillation, where the Pacific climate cycles between warm (El Niño, or little boy) and cool (La Niña, or little girl).

referred to as the climate event of the 20th century, penguin numbers dropped by 65 per cent.

Why worry about an event that happened 25 years ago? Scientists who build climate models for the future reckon that El Niños as strong as the one in 1997–1998 will come more often, with less time in between for wildlife to bounce back.*

*As this book heads out to the printer, a big 2023–24 El Niño season is expected. Be a scientist: do some research to see what impact it has had.

DANIEL PROAÑO AND PROJECT LIFE CHANGE

Teacher Daniel Proaño is the president of Fundación Un Cambio por la Vida (Project Life Change), and the co-founder, with Sophia Cooke, of Co-Galápagos. 'A big problem is the quality of access to the internet,' he says, emphasising how hard it is for students to get online. The potential solution is an example of the projects led by Co-Galápagos: a plan to create an intranet (a computer network) for schools, with a digital library that can be accessed by all.

DE-TRASHING THE PLACE

Juan Pablo Muñoz-Pérez, of the Galápagos Science Centre, takes an unusual approach to waste. He sees it as data that exposes pollution sources – and that can help eliminate them. While most tourists visiting the islands don't see much waste, he says that's because they spend little time on the windward sides of the islands, where conditions are rougher. Years ago, islanders relied on these beaches for the wood that washed up there. Now plastic drifts in, as well.

'It's shocking that you go to the most pristine, off-limits places in the islands, where there's no tourism, no fishing, isolated from everybody on the planet – and they are full of plastics,' JP says. 'The coast of the islands acts as a natural net for floating debris – much of it single-use plastic, such as drink bottles.'

There's more going on here than just clearing up waste. Plastics break down into tiny, microscopic particles that are swallowed by small sea creatures, then make their way up the food chain to top predators, including whales, sharks and humans.

While JP doesn't advocate getting rid of all plastics, eliminating single-use plastic could make a dent here – and everywhere else. He would like to make the Galápagos the first single-use-plastic-free place on Earth, and a model for the rest of the world.

SOPHIA COOKE, MAKING TEENS PART OF THE SOLUTION

Conservationist Sophia Cooke first came to the Galápagos from England to study an invasive bird species called the smooth-billed ani, then worked on the problem of feral cats (domestic cats living wild). She soon turned her attention to the broader ecosystem of the Galápagos, one that factors in the needs of people (another invasive species). Her objective is to improve communication between people studying the environment and those studying social issues – things like water, pollution, schools and family life – and to help get information about these things to leaders who are making decisions. Among the organisation's projects is one that combines taking teens diving to clean up plastic waste and teaching them to photograph their environment.

JP's team uses drones to map, log and analyse the plastic waste found on the shore. Walking the beach, they gather waste by the bagful and take it back to the lab to examine it closely. They're working to find out where the plastic came from and what industries might be the sources. Personal hygiene (such as toothbrushes)? Fishing (lines and nets)? Food and drink (bottles and wrappers)? While the plastics primarily come from South America, bottles from Japan and China show up, too. That's because a main source of waste is fishing fleets that fish just outside the Galápagos Marine Reserve.

As a result of the data JP's team has gathered, the Galápagos banned single-use plastics in 2015. Recently the ruling was extended to all of Ecuador. 'That's a big win,' says JP, who hopes Peru (another main source) will ban them, too, to help solve the problem of plastics on island shores and in the seas – declared the biggest issue for the oceans by the United Nations in 2021.

When you're super-protective of your shores, the way Galapagueños are, it's hard to see them damaged – and harder still to see hermit crabs tucking themselves into plastic 'shells'. Researchers are working to figure out where the trash came from so they can stop it at the source.

HARMONY AND BALANCE

We spent our last full day in the Galápagos Islands in Puerto Ayora, Santa Cruz, a busy town alive with music, flowers, restaurants, traffic and souvenir shops. We strolled around, watching pelicans begging at the market, peeking into SCUBA shops and joining a roaring crowd around a badminton match in the central park. Franklin's 12-year-old daughter, off from school for the day, accompanied our group's tour of the Charles Darwin Research Station at Academy Bay, and pointed out the wheelbarrows of native plants cut to feed the tortoises. She can already spot the differences between tortoises from one island and those from another.

The future of the Galápagos Islands depends on balancing a triangle of human and animal needs. In the first corner, the animals need clean water, plenty of food and space to migrate, mate and nest with minimum interference. In the second corner are tourists, who see the islands as a paradise of exotic vistas, once-in-a-lifetime animal sightings and beautiful beaches. In the third corner are human residents – Galapagueños, fellow citizens from Ecuador and scientists and other researchers.

The United Nations has designated the Galápagos a Sustainable Development Goals territory. This makes it a centre for trying to meet worldwide goals on a local scale, including protecting life, local food and water supply, and finding ways to help Galapagueños meet local goals first.

To scientists like Sophia and JP, the Galápagos Islands, so separate from everywhere else, allow for science experiments that let them get at the heart of difficult situations like pollution, water use, animal welfare and even how to bring back species from the brink of extinction. They hope that what they learn will help the islands' community come up with a plan for life in harmony with nature that might work for other parts of Ecosystem Earth.

SEBASTIÁN PILLA AND THE SANTA CRUZ YOUTH COUNCIL

Sebastián Pilla heads the Santa Cruz Youth Advisory Council, where he works with secondary schoolers as they learn about and take action on the United Nations' worldwide sustainability development goals (SDGs), with the aim of encouraging a new generation to lead the Galápagos into better environmental and community health. His motto is that little people in a little place can create major change.

AN UPWARD LOOK

The morning we were set to leave the Galápagos Islands, the *San José* stopped at North Seymour Island. There, the magnificence of magnificent frigate birds and the incredibly blue dancing feet of the blue-footed boobies welcomed us to their nests. We kept a respectful distance, even when meeting birds that weren't frightened of us. Like so many other Galápagos species, they hadn't learned to be afraid of humans. Maybe they should have been. If only they had known about the pollution, the fossil fuels, the invasive species that the human race had subjected them to. But no, these animals were responding to just our individual actions – our gentle tiptoeing around their nesting areas, the respect we showed by keeping our hands to ourselves. (Yes, we were well-fed and didn't need to eat them.) I'm idealistic enough to hope the birds knew we meant well.

JP feels optimistic about the future of the Galápagos because he is raising a daughter here. To him, every child who lives here, or visits the islands, or reads about them, will see them as something to be cherished – and take their story home. 'That could change the planet,' he says.

Not many places around the planet have the pride one Galapagueño shows in having 'Made in Galápagos' tattooed across his chest. It helps to have so many international visitors who are wowed by the place, but Galapagueños themselves recognise the specialness of their islands and the animal inhabitants.

It's late spring, early summer on the equator, the time of year when baby marine iguanas hatch. Young and foolish, they wind up running around San Cristóbal, because it's close to the beach. But let just one tiny iguana cross the road, and the bustling town halts. Everyone stops their cars. All the traffic lines up. People run into the road, shooing the baby to safety.

    It's the kind of thing that drives home what treasures these islands are, how unique their wildlife is and how much people care for them. It's the kind of story that gives a human like me hope, not just for the Galápagos, but for the world that is the setting for this jewel.

GLOSSARY

ADAPTIVE RADIATION
a process of evolution in which a species branches out to different niches in the environment, leading to variations in characteristics and the development of new species

'A'Ā LAVA
lava that cools as bubbles and pillows that collapse into holes and chunks. It is rough and difficult to walk on.

ARCHIPELAGO
group of islands such as the Galápagos or the British Isles

BIODIVERSITY
the variety of life in the world or in a particular place. High biodiversity means a place has lots of species.

BIOMASS
the total weight of a specific kind of living thing or all living things in a particular area

CALDERA
a bowl-shaped area that forms at the top of a volcano as lava flows out of it

CANNERY
a factory for processing food such as fish and sealing it into cans so that it can be shipped and stored for long periods of time before eating

CHEMOSYNTHESIS
a process in which living things make energy from chemicals in the environment. Hydrothermal vents in the deep sea are chemosynthetic ecosystems.

COLONY
a group of members of one species that live together and cooperate in some way

CONSERVATION
efforts made to preserve an area in its natural state

CRATER
a big hole caused by the impact of flying rock or a volcanic eruption

CURRENT
a river of water within a larger body of water such as an ocean. The water in a current acts differently from the water around it. For example, a current might have a different speed, temperature or direction of movement.

DNA
an abbreviation for deoxyribonucleic acid, DNA is the structure that codes for the building and operating of our bodies and the bodies of all living things.

ENDANGERED
found in smaller numbers than previously, and at risk of extinction

ENDEMIC
naturally occurring in a specific place

EVOLUTION
a process by which living things such as animals and plants change in response to their environments

EXTINCT
no longer in existence

FISHERY
an area where fish are caught or farmed to sell for food

FISHING HOLE
an area in the ocean, lake, river or stream where fish tend to be found

FLEET
a group of ships that are sailing together, doing the same thing, and often owned by the same person or company

GILLS
an organ found in fish that lets them take in oxygen from the water

HOT SPOT
a plume of magma that stays in place as a tectonic plate moves over it. This creates a chain of volcanoes that rise one by one to form islands.

HYDROTHERMAL VENT
a crack in the seafloor that emits heat from the magma below, giving rise to chemosynthetic ecosystems. (see *Chemosynthesis*)

INDIGENOUS
existing in a place before humans (or humans from elsewhere) first arrived there

INVASIVE
imported (on purpose or accidentally) from elsewhere, an invasive species reproduces quickly, causing trouble in its new environment.

LAGOON
a shallow body of water near and connected to a large body of water such as the ocean

LAVA
melted (molten) rock when it emerges from the Earth's crust as volcanoes. When it is inside the crust, it is called magma.

LAVA TUBE
a tunnel of solidified lava that forms when a channel of molten lava drains

MAGMA
melted (molten) rock under the Earth's crust

MARINE
having to do with the ocean

METABOLISM
the process by which our cells (and the cells of other living things) break down food to provide energy for the body

NATIVE
naturally occurring in a particular place

NICHE
the specific environment in which a species finds the food, water and other things (including other living things) it needs to live

PĀHOEHOE LAVA
lava that cools in ropey shapes

PARASITE
a living thing that lives on or in another living thing and takes its food from its host

PHOTOSYNTHESIS
process in which organisms get energy from the Sun. Most of Earth, including the surface of the ocean, is a photosynthetic environment.

PIT CRATER
a sinkhole formed when molten lava drains from an underground pocket

PLANKTON
tiny living things, some so small you need a microscope to see them, that live floating in the sea

SCUBA
swimming below the surface of the water using an oxygen tank and regulator (which controls the pressure of air in the lungs, matching it to the pressure of the sea at depth). The word scuba stands for Self-Contained Underwater Breathing Apparatus.

SEAMOUNT
undersea volcano that causes upwelling and forms a habitat for diverse species

SNORKELLING
swimming at or near the surface using a breathing tube. Snorkellers must stay near the surface in order to breathe.

SONAR
a device that allows a user to 'see' an area that is invisible to the eye by bouncing sound waves off of it and mapping the returning echoes

SPORE
a tiny cell produced by a plant or fungus, which can go on to develop into an adult of its species

SUBMERSIBLE
a small vehicle designed to travel underwater. A submersible may have a crew on board or be controlled remotely, in which case it is known as a remotely operated vehicle (ROV).

TECTONIC PLATES
enormous slabs of the Earth's crust that lie under the continents and oceans. Their movements, fuelled by the molten magma they sit atop, rips and rolls the Earth's crust in slow motion, leading to volcanoes and earthquakes, and even creating giant mountain chains such as the Himalaya.

UPWELLING
a process in which cold, nutrient-rich water is forced up from the seafloor, providing food to many species as it makes its way towards the surface

ZODIAC
a type of inflatable boat

WHALING STATION
a location where the carcasses of dead whales are carved up and processed

SOURCE NOTES

This book was developed through extensive research, interviews with scientists in the Galápagos Islands, reviews by experts in the archipelago, as well as my own travel notes. It would be impossible to list all the sources used, but here are some places to look for more information about the gorgeous Galápagos.

- Karen Romano Young

....

Berry, Kate, Juan-Pablo Muñoz-Pérez et al. 'The Mystery of a Marine Monster: Morphological and Performance Modifications in the World's Only Marine Lizard, the Galápagos Marine Iguana', *The Biological Journal of the Linnean Society*. bioRxiv preprint, Research Gate, https://www.researchgate.net/publication/341444560_The_Mystery_of_a_Marine_Monster_Morphological_and_Performance_Modifications_in_the_World%27s_only_Marine_Lizard_the_Galapagos_Marine_Iguana

Arnold, Marsha Diane, *Galapagueña* (Galápagos Girl) is the story of Valentina Cruz, who grew up to be a naturalist and park ranger. Illustrated by Angela Dominguez. Children's Book Press, 2023.

'Galapagueña' video. https://www.youtube.com/watch?v=jYpUerYjm4Q

Bulion, Leslie. *Galápagos*. Penguin Random House, 2023.

California Academy of Sciences Galápagos Islands Research. https://www.calacademy.org/learn-explore/scientific-expeditions/galapagos-islands-research

Center for Galápagos Studies, University of North Carolina. https://galapagos.unc.edu

Charles Darwin Foundation website, darwinfoundation.org

Cho, Lisa. *Galápagos Islands: Trip of a Lifetime*. Avalon Travel, 2018.

Cole, Joanna. *The Magic School Bus Explores Human Evolution*, illustrated by Bruce Degen. Scholastic, 2021

Fitter, Julian. *Wildlife of the Galápagos*. Princeton University Press, 2016.

Galápagos Conservancy, galapagos.org

Galápagos Science Centre, galapagosscience.org

Jackson, Tom. *Galápagos, Earth's Extraordinary Places*. Dorling Kindersley, 2022.

Keller, Michael. *Charles Darwin's On the Origin of Species: A Graphic Adaptation*, illustrated by Nicolle Racer Fuller. Rodale, 2009

Nicholls, Henry. *The Galápagos: A Natural History*. Basic Books, 2014

'Plastic in Paradise,' *The Guardian*, 3 April 2019. https://www.youtube.com/watch?v=aS8IBxi2xJE

'Spectacular Wildlife in the Galápagos Islands,' film. https://www.youtube.com/watch?v=Z3wNjM1Dnsc

Stewart, Paul D. *Galápagos: The Islands That Changed the World*. Yale University Press, 2007.

INDEX

A
'A'ā lava 11
adaptation 29, 30, 32
adaptive radiation 32
Alcedo Volcano 42
alternative energy 52
archaeology 36

B
Ballard, Bob 12, 13, 14, 15
Baltra Island 6, 48
Beck, Rollo 36
biodiversity 16–17
breeding programmes 44, 45

C
calderas 10, 11
Carnegie Ridge 9
Cayot, Linda 45
climate change 52–3
Cocos-Galápagos Swimway 25
conservation 44–7, 48–9, 50–1
Cooke, Sophia 53, 54, 57
coral reefs 22, 52
cormorants, flightless 18
COVID-19 pandemic 50
crabs, 13, 15, 25, 55
craters 10
creation 31
crust, Earth's 9, 20
Cueva del Cascajo 8
Cunninghame, Francesca 39
currents, ocean 20, 22

D
Darwin, Charles 28, 30–1, 35, 36
Darwin Volcano 29
desalination 35
DNA 33

E
ecosystems 44, 50
educational initiatives 50, 51, 53, 57
El Niño events 33, 52–3
endangered species 17, 39, 41, 44, 57
endemic species 17, 34, 44
environmental concerns 50–1, 54–5
Española Island 9
evolution 31, 33, 36
extinctions 31, 36, 40, 41, 46, 57

F
Fernanda 46–7
Fernandina Island 9, 10–11, 18, 20, 26, 43, 46
Fessl, Birgit 39
finches 29, 30–3, 39
fish aggregating devices (FADs) 23
fish/fishing 17, 18, 22, 23, 24, 39, 50, 52
Floreana Island 35, 37, 41
food chain 12, 23, 30, 54

G
Galápagos Ecological Airport 5, 48
Galápagos Marine Reserve 23, 49–50, 55
Galápagos National Park 4, 8, 49
Galápagos Rift 9, 49
genetics 32, 33
global warming 50, 52
goats 42–4
Grant, Peter and Rosemary 32–3
Guaranda, Franklin 6–7, 9, 18, 28, 56

H
habitats 16
Heyerdahl, Thor 36–9
hot spots 9, 11
humans, arrival of 34–9, 42, 44
hybrids 46
hydrothermal vents 12–13, 15

I
iguanas 18, 26–7, 58–9
indigenous species 17
internet access 53
invasive species 39, 42–4, 54, 58
Isabela Island 18, 28, 29, 39, 42–5
island formation 9

L
La Cumbre (The Top) 10
lava 10, 11, 42
lava tubes 8, 18
Lonesome George 41, 46–7
Los Gemelos (The Twins) 8

MNO
magma 9
mapping, seafloor 20, 21
migration 25, 35
Mission Blue 25
Muñoz-Pérez, Juan Pablo 27, 54, 57, 58
natural selection 29, 30–1, 33
niches 32, 42
Nieto, Ainoa 47
North Seymour Island 58
Ocean Exploration Trust Corps 12
Ozouville, Noemi d' 51

P
Pacific Ocean 11, 12, 33, 36, 52
pāhoehoe lava 11
Pazmiño Jaramillo, Diana Alexandra 24, 51
penguins, Galápagos 18, 19, 52
photosynthesis 12
Pilla, Sebastián 57
Pinta Island 41, 46–7
pit craters 8
plastic waste 54–5
pollution 50, 54–5, 58
predators 18, 27, 32, 39, 41, 42
Proaño, Daniel 53

R
Ramirez-González, Jorge 23
Reichenbach, María José 50
Ring of Fire 11
Rose Garden 12–15

S
Salinas de León, Pelayo 21, 25
San Cristóbal Island 52, 59
Santa Cruz Island 8, 40, 56, 57
Santa Fe Island 41
satellite, tracking by 25, 47
scientific research 36, 39, 48–9, 56, 57
sea level, rising 52
seamounts 20, 21, 23
settlers, early 36–9
sharks 8, 18, 19, 23–5
sinkholes 8
sonar 14, 21
Soule, Adam 20, 21
sustainability 49, 50, 57

T
tectonic plates 9, 11
tortoises, giant 29, 30, 34, 35, 40–7
tourism 39, 44, 48–9, 50, 54, 56
tubeworms, giant 13, 14, 15

UVW
UNESCO World Heritage Site 49–50
upwelling 20
volcanoes 9, 10, 11, 20, 42, 46
waste 54–5
whales/whaling 18, 35
Wolf Volcano 29, 42, 46

ABOUT THE AUTHOR AND ILLUSTRATOR

KAREN ROMANO YOUNG

Karen Romano Young is a writer, illustrator, science communicator and polar explorer. She has written more than two dozen books for children, including Try This!, Mission: Sea Turtle Rescue, Shark Quest and Antarctica: The Melting Continent. She is a veteran of ten ocean science research voyages, including dives to the bottom of the sea. Karen lives in the woods of Connecticut, USA, with her husband and a big furry dog.

AMY GRIMES

Amy Grimes is a Bristol-based illustrator who graduated from Camberwell College of Art in 2014 with a first in Illustration. Particularly inspired by nature and the patterns found there, Amy's bright and bold illustrations feature botanical motifs and leafy landscapes. She draws on an iPad and also hand-paints textures, which she scans and works into her illustrations to create digital collages.

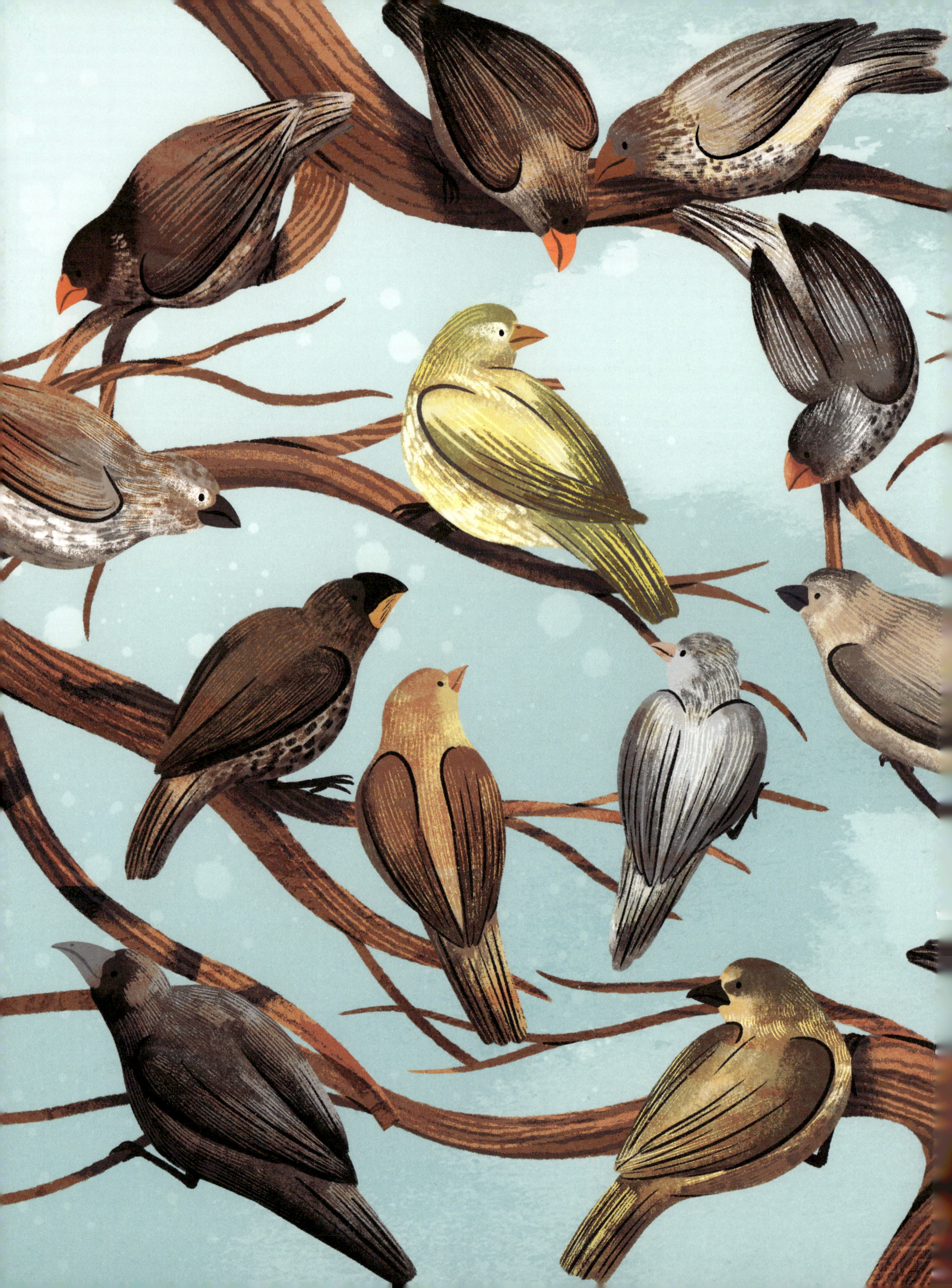